# FULL SEASON ACADEMY TRAINING PROGRAM

## U9-12

## 40 Sessions (200 Practices) from Italian Serie 'A' Coaches

WRITTEN BY

MIRKO MAZZANTINI     &     SIMONE BOMBARDIERI

PUBLISHED BY

# FULL SEASON ACADEMY TRAINING PROGRAM

## U9-12

## 40 Sessions (200 Practices) from Italian Serie 'A' Coaches

**First Published July 2013 by SoccerTutor.com**

Info@soccertutor.com | www.SoccerTutor.com

**UK:** 0208 1234 007 | **US:** (305) 767 4443 | **ROTW:** +44 208 1234 007
**ISBN:** 978-0-9576705-1-8

### Authors
Mirko Mazzantini and Simone Bombardieri © 2013

### Edited by
Alex Fitzgerald - SoccerTutor.com

### Cover Design by
Alex Macrides, Think Out Of The Box Ltd.
Email: design@thinkootb.com Tel: +44 (0) 208 144 3550

### Diagrams
Diagram designs by SoccerTutor.com. All the diagrams in this book have been created using SoccerTutor.com Tactics Manager Software available from *www.SoccerTutor.com*

Note: While every effort has been made to ensure the technical accuracy of the content of this book, neither the author nor publishers can accept any responsibility for any injury or loss sustained as a result of the use of this material.

# Soccer Italian Style Coaches

**Mirko Mazzantini**
ACF Fiorentina
Academy Coach

Mirko Mazzantini coached at Empoli FC for 10 years, working with all the main age groups at academy level. In 2010 he was recruited by AFC Fiorentina to work with the U14/U15 Academy teams.

During the 2010/11 season Mirko won the U15 Italian Academy Serie 'A' championship.

In 2011/12 Mirko was the Assistant of the Fiorentina Reserve team during pre-season and he was the coach of the ACF Fiorentina U14 team who won the Academy Serie 'A' championship and some international tournaments.

Mirko is currently the ACF Fiorentina U15 coach for the 2012/13 season.

He is a qualified football coach through the "Young Players Coach" program and a UEFA 'B' Licenced Coach, as well as an author of many coaching publications, articles, books and DVDs.

**Simone Bombardieri**
Empoli FC
Academy Coach

Simone Bombardieri played for Empoli FC for 5 years. He then started his career as a coach for the club 15 years ago at the age of 22, where he has been coaching various academy age groups from U9-U14.

In the 2011/12 season, Simone was the coach of the Empoli FC U14 team who reached the final of the Nick Cup International Tournament, where they lost in extra time against Inter Milan. They also finished eighth in the Academy Serie 'A' championship.

Simone is currently the Empoli FC U15 coach for the 2012/13 season.

He is also a qualified football coach through the "Young Players Coach" program and a UEFA 'B' Licenced Coach, as well as an author of many coaching publications, articles, books and DVDs.

**Tommaso Tanini**
ACF Fiorentina
Academy Coach

We would like to give a special thanks to Tommaso Tanini for helping us produce this book. Tommaso has coached at Empoli FC for 11 years. Tommaso is now the Fitness Coach for the Fiorentina U15 team.

He is also a UEFA 'B' Licenced Coach.

# Soccer Italian Style

## SOCCER ITALIAN STYLE IS WORLDWIDE...WORK WITH US!

**SOCCER ITALIAN STYLE** has organised youth football events in many countries around the world. If you are a Club Executive, a Coach, a Technical Director or just an individual passionate about the sport and you want your players to have a unique experience, please contact us or visit our website: www. SoccerItalianStyle.it

**PROFESSIONAL ITALIAN CAMP** is a week of football for boys and girls aged 6 to 18 years old. It is where fun meets the training methodologies of the best Italian academies and is taught by experienced staff who have worked with with some of highest level clubs in Italy.

**PROFESSIONAL ITALIAN TEAM CAMP** is a weekly team training camp with the work planned around a highly professional methodology which is tested continuously, innovated and adapted based on the level and characteristics of the participating team.

**SOCCER ITALIAN STYLE COACHING CLINICS** are organised for all different levels and are based on a proven model that creates lots of interest and enjoyment for the participants. The time spent in the classroom is filled with numerous videos from professional training sessions in Italy and it is supported by on-field demonstrations of the concepts discussed.

**NEW INITIATIVE: SOCCER AND TOURISM IN ITALY:** Soccer Italian Style has a partnership with an important travel agency to provide a unique experience: improve as a player and sightsee the best parts of Tuscany. Firenze, Pisa, Lucca, Siena, and 5 Terre are just some of the magnificent places waiting for you.

If you want your team to have a week of highly professional training and at the same time be immersed in the culture of Italy, Soccer Italian Style can plan your trip in detail, adapting the itinerary and lodging based on the wishes and needs of the players and chaperones.

# The Italian Style Story

Soccer Italian Style was founded in 2005 by 2 passionate professional coaches, Mirko Mazzantini and Simone Bombardieri. Since their first trip overseas, the young coaches' goal has been to share their experiences with passion and professionalism.

The Soccer Italian Style network has spread quickly to many continents through various partnerships, working with youth football clubs, youth football associations and businesses that distribute sports books and videos.

In 2011 Mirko Mazzantini and Simone Bombarideri had the honour to present a lesson at the Coverciano Coaches Training Centre organised by the Italian Football Federation.

Mirko and Simone have received recognition from many countries, and this is reflected in themany contacts and collaborations they have established and by the success of the products developed. This has led to Mirko and Simone visiting many countries throughout the world to share their expertise, particularly in the USA, Canada, Norway, Japan, Australia, New Zealand and many Asian countries. The success enjoyed by Soccer Italian Style has encouraged the founders to increase their efforts with new developments to complement the existing products.

All the initiatives focus on the common denominator; the working philosophy of Soccer Italian Style, as well as the result of personal experiences in professional football clubs, trips around the world and personal experiences.

Numerous coaches, club directors and football fans continuously contact the staff through the website:

**www.SoccerItalianStyle.it**

As a result of this interest, Mirko and Simone have welcomed other professional coaches and athletic trainers to their football family to help meet the needs of all that are interested.

# Contents

# Introduction

The training sessions proposed in this book are based on the principle of specialisation, which consists on focusing on one main technical objective in each session.

Besides the main technical objective, a coordination objective is developed connected to the main objective together with secondary technical objectives. The intent of this model is to develop sessions that are complete and logical for the development of the player.

The structure of the session is the same in all of the sessions and only the content changes.

The session is divided into the following blocks:

### Warm up game
This is of a short duration (10 mins) and it is a fun activity to allow the players to unwind from the stress and pressures they have had during the day.

### Coordination exercise
During this activity we work on the coordination ability associated with the main technical objective.

### Skill exercise
This activity is aimed at teaching and correcting the main technical gesture.

### Game situation
During this activity the main technical gesture is applied to the various situations that players face in a real game scenario. We start with the simplest situations of 1v1 to more complex situations.

### Game with a theme
The game with a theme reproduces a situation similar to a game, with the introduction of a series of rules aimed to force the players to apply and work on the objectives of the session.

### Free game
This is the moment of the game that is free of specific rules, where we could introduce some simple and basic concepts of collective tactics.

The 34 sessions are divided into 7 different training units (juggling, running with the ball, passing, shooting, heading, throw-ins and receiving). They are sufficient to run a complete year program for the U9-12 age category.

The model of planning presented in this book is only one example of the many combinations of sessions that a coach could run during the year.

One suggestion that we would like to give is that together with the principle of specialisation the coach takes into consideration the principle of progression, to plan the training sessions in a way to put the player in the condition to learn from the more simple to the complex. This principle should always be present in the coach's mind when planning the sessions and this is the principle we have adopted in our plans.

It is evident that the coach can always increase the level of difficulty when he thinks it appropriate, for example by reducing the time of execution of a technical gesture, or by decreasing the space available to the players.

In addition to the specific technical sessions you can find sessions on the motor-coordination abilities. These additional plans are focused on improving the coordination of the players, considered the foundation for mastering technique.

We have also prepared a table that shows the correlation between the technical skill and coordination abilities.

The work ends with an analysis of the social-psychological aspect of the age category by Doctor Cioni. It is very important for a coach to know the issues faced by this age group in order to deal with them during the course of the season.

*Mirko Mazzantini*
*Simone Bombardieri*
*Tommaso Tanini*

# CHAPTER
## 1

# Physiological, Social And Psychological Development In Players From 9 To 12 Years Old

# Growth Maturation: Physical Growth

Puberty is a period of fast physical and physiological growth but not just that. It is also a period where the individual's expectations of social interaction take a different role than they used to.

When does puberty start? It is difficult to answer with certainty as it different for each person. Using a wide range we can frame puberty between the ages of 8 and 14. With more clarity, if we do not take into consideration the early and late developers, we can say puberty starts between the age of 9 and 13 years old.

Females usually start puberty earlier than males and 4 or 5 years after the first signs, the puberty modifications tend to finish their cycle.

Given the nature of this book, it is important to focus the attention on how the physical maturation affects the development of an individual's personality in general.

The quick physical changes that accompany puberty make it difficult for the individual to establish a coherent interior feeling; therefore the individual requires some time to integrate these changes with the identity that is slowly developing.

The first effect on personality is that most adolescents do not grow at the same rate as the rest of boys and girls of the same age. Some think they are too tall, too short, too skinny or too fat. Some are not happy with their nose or their own legs, etc.

This is one of the psychological problems connected with the physical development, many adolescents are not satisfied with their own physical conditions and this creates anxiety.

Moreover, the adult does not understand how important this is for the individual, which adds to conflicts and incomprehension.

Another aspect to consider in connection with puberty is the modification of body parts proportions. The head, hands and feet are the first parts to reach the adult size, but the arms and legs grow slower compared to the main body. These unbalances explain the temporary loss of coordination experienced by some adolescents, particularly those who grow rapidly.

For a short period of time the individuals perceive their hands or feet to be too big. Their disharmony may be accentuated from comments made by adults as well.

As mentioned, when the physical growth is accelerated, there is a loss of the coordination abilities (these abilities had reached a good level at the end of the age of 10). This aspect has also a negative effect on self-esteem.

# Intellectual Growth

Between the age of 9 and 12 the following cognitive abilities start to develop:

## 1. Quantitative

Individuals solve intellectual problems easier, quicker and more effectively.

## 2. Qualitative

The mental processes used to define problems and then think them over are modified considerably.

In this period, the phase of development of the mental structures starts, the use of formal thought.

Formal thought consists of the ability to conduct thoughts in a logical manner, without the necessity to start the thought from a direct experience and verify the conclusion of the thought through a direct experience.

This ability allows the adolescent to use notions like infinite, probabilities, chance, etc.

The formation of the stage connected to the formal operations allows to develop the ability to think in a more abstract way (hypothetical thought), to formulate hypothesis, to test them, verify and think what can happen (not anymore just what it is).

These changes have enormous implications, for example, conflicts may arise with parents because the adolescent discovers they do not behave the same way as their parents have taught the values of life, and up to that point the parents had been considered as role models.

At the same time, adolescents are very critical of social, political and religious systems. This is to be attributed to the development of the operative formal thought.

The stage of formal operations is characterised by a careful analysis of themselves, thought and behaviour appear egocentric and because the adolescents think a lot about themselves, they also believe that other people always criticise their thoughts, feelings, behaviours and physical appearance.

# Social development

The adolescent grows into an adult in gradual stages, in order to adapt to the maturation during puberty, reach independence from their parents and establish relationships with their peers. He or she must also elaborate a philosophy of life and a sense of personal identity.

The relationship with the parents is characterised by intense conflicts. Many of the problems derive from the dimension of 'authority and subordination.' The adolescent does not accept the principle of authority anymore, is able to use the formal thought and expects a reason for any decision made by the parents.

By facing these conflicts and growing crises the adolescent acquires their own personal and social identity.

The relationship with teachers changes as well. From a professional study (Petter, 1990) the relationship is characterised by tension, anxiety and resentment. The adolescent requires more recognition, and if they are entrusted and empowered they are motivated to improve themselves.

The relationship with peers is very important. Friendships become more intimate, exclusive and long lasting. At this stage friendship is not only based on the activities exercised together but also on mutual respect.

In the relationship of friendship there is room for expression and the sharing of life experiences or feelings.

The inclusion in the group is very important in this period. It is through the participation within groups that adolescents can find the need for a social identity.

Being in groups allows adolescents to get to know themselves and others. He or she can learn to deal with individuals of the opposite sex in a protected environment, the can relate to older friends who have the same interests and consider them role models (more so than with an adult).

The social game becomes important. With the development of the formal thought, adolescents are able to play games with more complex rules, like cards and chess. And sports have the function of enjoyment, allowing the individual to live, even if at a symbolic level, the problems and conflicts arising in the day to day life.

Sport can be very important for an individual for social challenges, a means for the formation and control of their identity.

Reference:

Paul H. Mussen, John J. Conger, Kerome Kagan, Aletha C. Huston: *The Formation of the Child and the Personality, Zanichelli*

R. Vianello: *Psychology of development, Junior Edition*

# CHAPTER

## 2

# Training Session Format

# Outline of Training Sessions

We have split up our sessions into Training Units. This allows us to focus on one specific training objective at a time, which we have found to be the most effective way of training this age group.

**This is how the Training Units are organised:**

**Running with the Ball** - 5 Sessions

**Passing** - 10 Sessions

**Shooting** - 9 Sessions

**Heading** - 3 Sessions

**Receiving** - 5 Sessions

**Juggling** - 1 Session

**Throw-ins** - 1 Session

**We also have additional Motor Skills Units in the last chapter:**

**Differentiation** - 5 Practices

**Reactions** - 6 Practices

**Adaptation and Transformation** - 6 Practices

**Space and Orientation** - 6 Practices

**Rhythm** - 3 Practices

**Motor Combinations** - 6 Practices

**Balance** - 2 Practices

**All of these 34 sessions are formed like this:**

| First Game/Warm Up | 10 mins |
|---|---|
| Coordination | 5 or 10 mins |
| Technical | 15 or 20 mins |
| Game situation | 15 mins |
| Game with a Theme | 20 mins |
| Final game/Small Side Game | 20 mins |

# Practice Format

Each practice in the sessions includes clear diagrams with supporting training notes:

- Name of Practice
- Objective of Practice
- Description
- Variations/Progressions (if applicable)
- Coaching Points

# Key

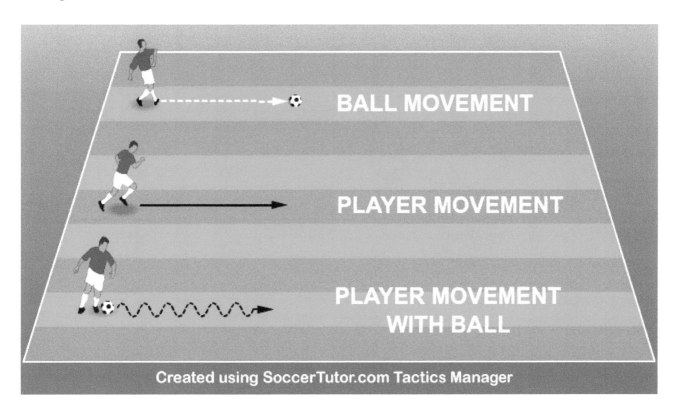

# CHAPTER

## 3

# Running With The Ball Training Unit

**Primary Technical objective:** Running with the ball.

**Coordination Objective:** Quickness, adaptation, transformation, rhythm and motor combinations.

**Secondary Technical Objective:** Passing and shooting.

**Tactical Objective:** 1v1 Duels.

**Duration of Session:** 85-100 minutes

---

We recommend starting the session with exercises for general mobility to prevent injuries.

---

| Practice 1 | Running with the Ball - '4 Corners' | 10 mins |

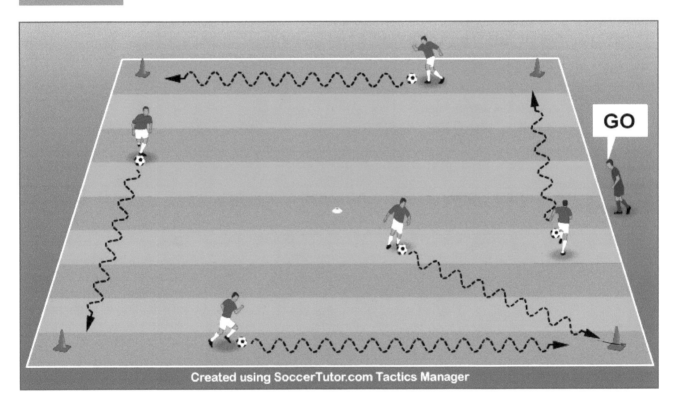

Created using SoccerTutor.com Tactics Manager

### Description

4 players are positioned in the corners of a 10 x 10 yard square with 1 player in the centre. On the coach's call, each player must move from their position and dribble the ball to another corner.

The player that is left without a corner position does not get a point and starts in the centre of the square forth next round.

### Variations

**1)** Dribble only with the right foot. **2)** Dribble only with the left foot. **3)** Dribble only with outside of the foot.

### Coaching Points

1. As this is competitive, players need to dribble the ball quickly, but also concentrate on maintaining good control.
2. Slowing down and stopping the ball in the corner is essential and can be demonstrated.
3. Players need to be aware of the movement of others to decide which corner to run to.

---

## Practice 2 | Ball Control and Coordination Relay | 5-10 mins

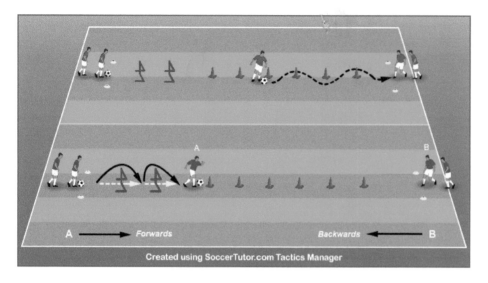

Created using SoccerTutor.com Tactics Manager

### Description

The first player must pass the ball under the hurdles and jump over them, dribble through the cones and finally give/pass the ball to the teammate opposite them (B).

Player B must do the same going backwards (cones first, hurdles second).

Make this a competition.

### Variations

**1)** Dribbling only with the right or left foot. **2)** Vary the distances between the cones.

### Coaching Points

1. Close control is important here so the players should use many touches.

2. There should be a soft feel with the ball.

## Practice 3 | Close Control with Shooting Accuracy | 10-15 mins

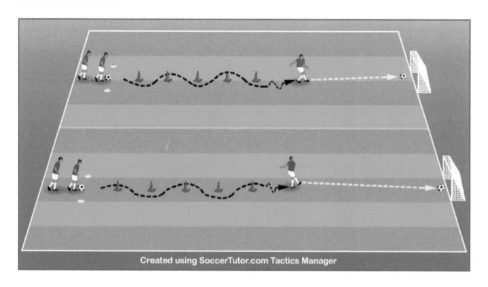

Created using SoccerTutor.com Tactics Manager

### Description

Players dribble through the cones and shoot in the small goals. Vary the sequence of dribbling through the cones and vary the distances between the cones.

Vary the type of ball and use different techniques of running with the ball.

### Variations

**1)** Dribbling only with the right or left foot. **2)** Dribbling only with the inside or outside of the feet.

### Coaching Points

1. It is necessary to have good control with soft touches at speed to dribble through cones without errors.

2. Players should have slightly bent knees when changing direction, with the ball close to their feet.

## Practice 4 — Coordination & Agility Training with 1v1 Duels — 15 mins

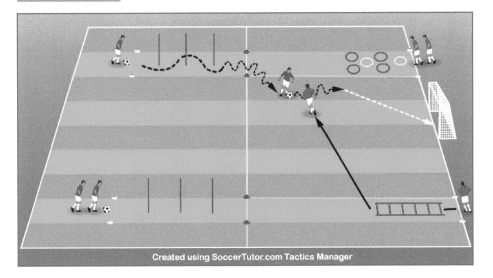

Created using SoccerTutor.com Tactics Manager

**Description**

The blue players dribble through the poles and then try to score a goal.

The red players work through a coordination course and then move to defend the goal.

Switch roles halfway through and the team that scores more goals win.

**Variations**

**1)** Play with a goalkeeper. **2)** Modify the coordination course. **3)** Dribble using different parts of the foot.

**Coaching Points**

1. Players should use soft touches to dribble through the poles, keeping the ball close to their feet.
2. Encourage players to use feints/moves to beat in the 1v1 duel.

## Practice 5 — 3v3 with End Zones Small Sided Game — 20 mins

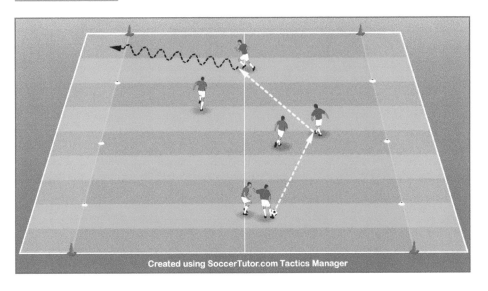

Created using SoccerTutor.com Tactics Manager

**Description**

We play 3v3 and the teams must dribble the ball into the end zone.

The goal is valid if the ball is dribbled beyond the end zone and stopped with the sole of the foot.

The team that scores the most goals in 3 minutes win a point.

**Variation**

Before being allowed to score a goal, the team must first complete 5 passes.

**Coaching Points**

1. Make sure players use all parts of their feet when dribbling the ball.
2. The players need quick movements to dominate the 1v1 situations and enter the end zone.

## Practice 6 — Free Small Sided Game — 20 mins

**Primary Technical objective:** Running with the ball and shielding the ball.

**Coordination Objective:** Quickness, adaptation, transformation, differentiation, motor combinations and balance.

**Secondary Technical Objective:** Passing and shooting.

**Tactical Objective:** 1v1 Duels.

**Duration of Session:** 85-100 minutes

We recommend starting the session with exercises for general mobility to prevent injuries.

---

**Practice 1**    **Dribbling and Shielding Warm Up - 'The Hunt'**    **10 mins**

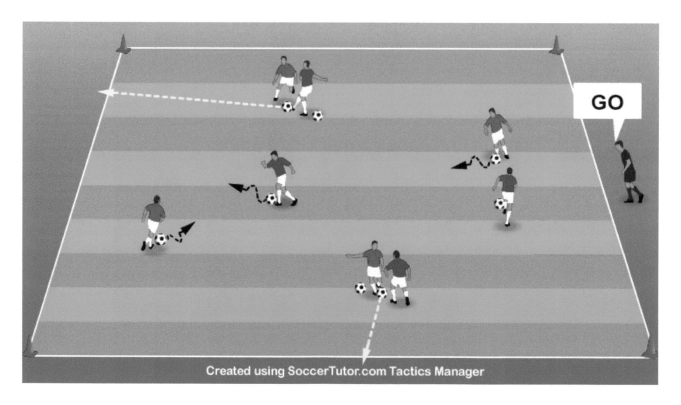

### Description

In a 20 x 20 yard square, there are 2 teams with every player in possession of a ball dribbling around freely.

The players wait for the coach's call, and when he shouts 'GO' the players have to try and kick their opponent's balls out of play (while maintaining control of their own).

The team that kicks all of their opposition's balls out of play first wins.

### Variation

Dribble only with right foot, dribble only with left foot, dribble only with outside of foot etc.

### Coaching Point

1. The correct body shape is required to shield the ball, making sure their body is a barrier between the opponent and the ball.

---

## Practice 2 Coordination Relay

**5-10 mins**

*Created using SoccerTutor.com Tactics Manager*

### Description

Players must dribble through the cones, stop the ball (leaving it) and do a forward roll.

They then run around the pole and then repeat the exercise back to their teammates (another forward roll and dribble through the cones). The next player then goes.

### Variations

**1)** Play with a goalkeeper. **2)** Modify the coordination course. **3)** Dribble using different parts of the foot.

### Coaching Points

1. Make the exercise a competition to increase the speed of play.
2. Accuracy when dribbling around the cones is key to save time keeping the ball close to their feet.

---

## Practice 3 Close Control, Move & Pass Exercise

**15-20 mins**

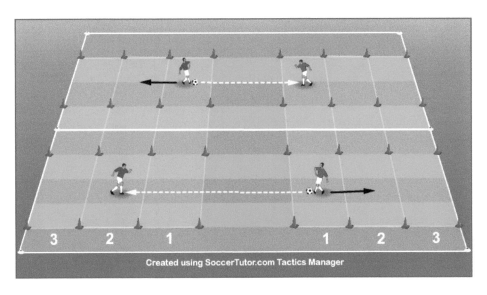

*Created using SoccerTutor.com Tactics Manager*

### Description

Players can be up to 20 yards apart from each other.

The first (blue) passes the ball from zone 1 to their teammate who is in their respective zone 1. After the pass the blue player moves to the next zone.

The red player then passes from zone 1 to the blue player who is now in their zone 2. The red player then moves back to their zone 2 to receive the next pass.

The same is done for zone 3.

### Variations

1. Make the players run and touch or turn around a cone before receiving.
2. Get the players to dribble the ball around a cone before passing the ball, thus working on running with the ball at the same time.

## Practice 4    Dribbling and Turning - '1v1 Pursuit'    **15 mins**

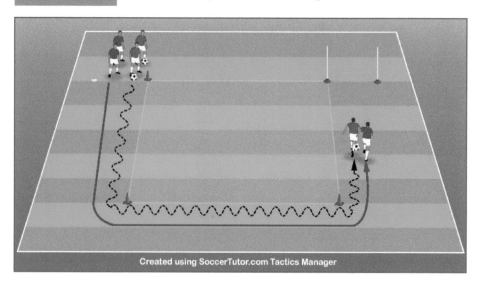

Created using SoccerTutor.com Tactics Manager

### Description

The player must dribble the ball around the cones as shown and get to the small goal/gate at the end.

The other player (blue) chases the red player without a ball and tries to prevent him from going through the goal/gate.

### Variations

**1)** Dribbling with the outside of the foot. **2)** With the inside of the foot. **3)** With just the left or right foot.

### Coaching Points

1. When running with the ball round corners, you need to slow down and bend the knees to change direction.

2. Players should use both feet and all parts of the feet when dribbling the ball.

---

## Practice 5    '4 Goals' 4v4 Small Sided Game    **20-25 mins**

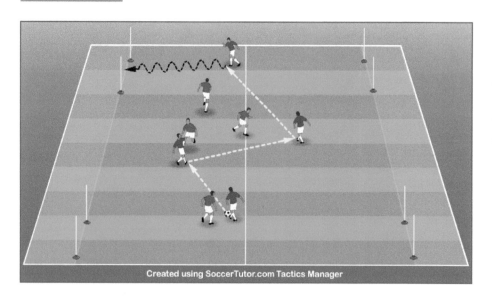

Created using SoccerTutor.com Tactics Manager

### Description

Here we play a free 4v4 small sided game.

The players score a goal if they are able to dribble the ball through one of the gates/goals.

### Variations

1. Tournament with more teams.

2. Players have to stop the ball on the line to score.

3. Limit the maximum amount of touches.

---

## Practice 6    Free Small Sided Game    **20 mins**

---

**Primary Technical objective:** Running with the ball and changes of direction.

**Coordination Objective:** Quickness, adaptation, transformation, motor combinations and balance.

**Secondary Technical Objective:** Passing and shooting.

**Tactical Objective:** 1v2 play.

**Duration of Session:** 85-100 minutes

We recommend starting the session with exercises for general mobility to prevent injuries.

---

| Practice 1 | Close Control and Turning with Shot | 10 mins |

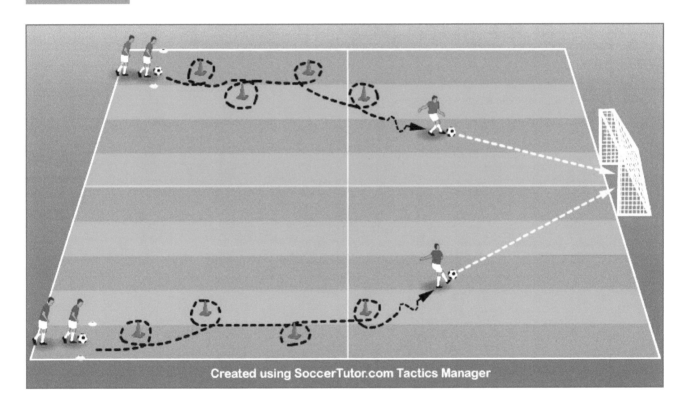

Created using SoccerTutor.com Tactics Manager

### Description

This is a competition between 2 teams. Each player must dribble and turn around the cones as shown in the diagram. They then shoot in the goal.

The players start at the same time and the first player to score a goal gets a point for their team. The next players then need to start at the same time (on the coach's call/whistle).

### Variations

1. Dribbling only with the right/left foot.
2. Dribbling only with the outside of the foot.

### Coaching Points

1. Players need to use very soft touches and all parts of the foot to turn tightly around the cones.
2. When shooting players should slow down and place their non-striking foot next to the ball.

---

## Practice 2  1v1 Duels - Dribbling & Changes of Direction    5-10 mins

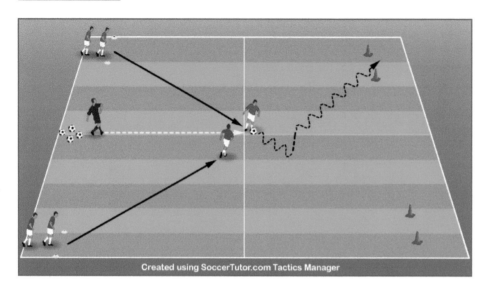

Created using SoccerTutor.com Tactics Manager

### Description
As soon as the coach passes the ball into the centre, 1 player from each team moves quickly to compete in a 1v1 duel and must dribble the ball through one of the 2 goals.

If the defender wins the ball he can score as well. Encourage the players to change direction as they can score in either of the 2 goals.

### Variation
Vary the starting positions (change the angles/distance).

### Coaching Point
1. When changing direction in 1v1 situations, players should drop their shoulder (feint) and slightly bend their knees to quickly change direction.

## Practice 3  Technical Ball Control & Changes of Direction    15-20 mins

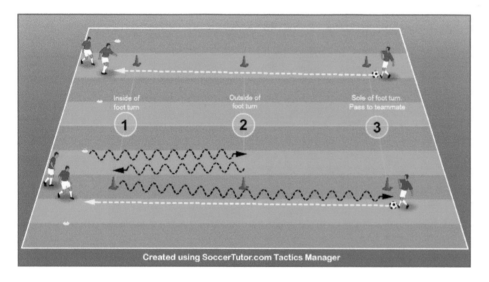

Inside of foot turn

Outside of foot turn

Sole of foot turn. Pass to teammate

Created using SoccerTutor.com Tactics Manager

### Description
*STAGE 1*
Dribble at maximum speed to the 2nd cone, quickly change direction with the outside of the foot and dribble back to the 1st cone.

*STAGE 2*
Quickly change direction again, this time with the inside of the foot and continue to the last cone.

*STAGE 3*
Quickly change direction again, this time using the sole of the foot and finish with a pass to teammate on the opposite side. The next player does the same.

### Variations
**1)** Switch the changes of direction. **2)** Introduce a shot on goal at the end.

### Coaching Points
1. Players need to slow down and bend the knees to change direction.
2. Keep the ball close to the feet when dribbling in tight areas.

## Practice 4    Dribbling Coordination and 1v2 Duel    15 mins

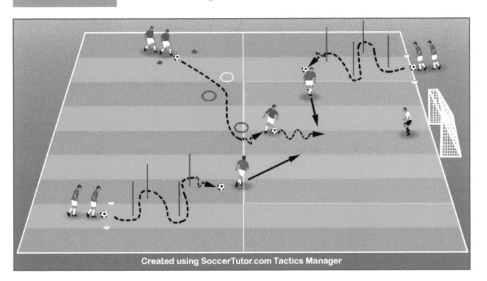

Created using SoccerTutor.com Tactics Manager

### Description

2 defenders (red) dribble the ball around the poles, leave the ball at the end of the course and run to defend the goal.

The blue player dribbles round the rings, and then quickly dribbles towards the goal trying to score past the goalkeeper in a 2v1 situation.

### Variations

**1)** Dribbling with the outside/inside of the foot. **2)** Switch sides. **3)** Dribble with left/right foot only.

### Coaching Points

1. Again, there needs to be soft touches and close control when dribbling through the obstacles.
2. Start with passive defenders and progress to them being fully active.

## Practice 5    4v4 (+GK) Attacking Combinations and Incisive Dribbling in and Around the Penalty Area    20-25 mins

Created using SoccerTutor.com Tactics Manager

### Description

The blue players outside the penalty area pass the ball around looking to find a channel/space to enter and attack the box trying to shoot and score a goal.

The 4 red players defend the goal. Change roles often.

### Variation

Play with the hands and shoot with a volley.

### Coaching Points

1. Awareness and good decision making is required to judge the right time to dribble into the box.
2. Players need to check away from their marker before moving to create space and receive the ball.

## Practice 6    Free Small Sided Game    20 mins

**Primary Technical objective:** Running with the ball and feints/moves to beat.

**Coordination Objective:** Quickness, adaptation, transformation and reactions.

**Secondary Technical Objective:** Changes of direction and shooting.

**Tactical Objective:** 1v1 play.

**Duration of Session:** 85-100 minutes

---

We recommend starting the session with exercises for general mobility to prevent injuries.

---

## Practice 1  Quick Reactions Dribbling Game                    10 mins

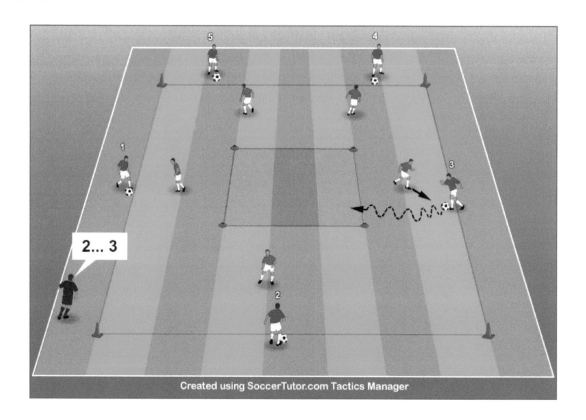

Created using SoccerTutor.com Tactics Manager

### Description

In an area 30 x 30 yards, the blue players are all on the outside with a ball each. The red players are on the inside of the square and must defend the inner box which is 7 x 7 yards.

On the coach's call, 1 blue player at a time tries to dribble the ball into the centre box (to score a point). The teams switch roles halfway through and the team with the most points wins.

### Variations

**1)** Dribbling with the outside of the feet. **2)** Dribble only with the right or left foot.

### Coaching Points

1.  Quick reactions are needed to dribble into the centre before the defender can position themselves.

2.  Use feints/moves to beat to take the ball past the defender.

---

---

**Practice 2**  **Dribbling Race with Turning and Shooting**  **5-10 mins**

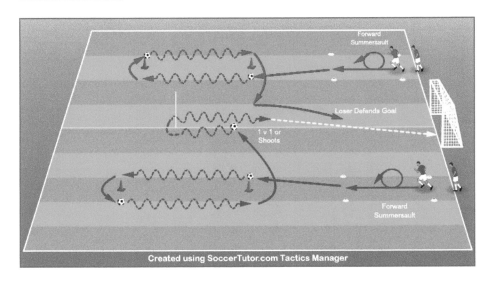

Created using SoccerTutor.com Tactics Manager

### Description

In this practice, 2 teams are racing. The red and blue players start at the same time and must do a forward roll, take the ball and dribble round the blue cone as shown and then dribble back, stopping the ball with their sole.

The 2 players then both try to run and get to the ball in the middle first.

The first player to get to the ball in the middle dribbles around the pole and shoots at goal, while the other player becomes the goalkeeper.

### Variations

**1)** Dribbling with the outside of the feet. **2)** Dribble with only right or left foot.

### Coaching Point

Quick reactions and rhythm are required for the transitions to the different sections of the practice (Roll → Dribble → Turn → Sprint → 1v1 → Shoot).

---

**Practice 3**  **Dribbling with Quick Changes of Direction**  **15-20 mins**

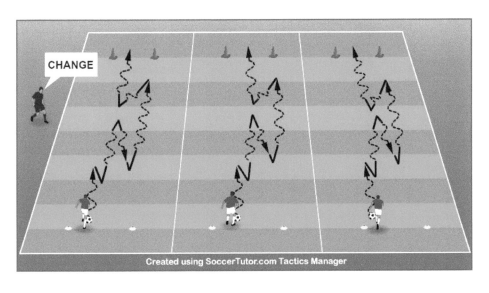

Created using SoccerTutor.com Tactics Manager

### Description

Players are divided into 3 groups with 1 player per group starting at the same time.

Players dribble with quick changes of direction at the command of the coach using the inside of the foot.

At the coach's final call, the players dribble quickly through the cones.

### Variation

Change of direction with the outside of the foot.

### Coaching Points

1. Players need to keep the ball close to their feet, so they can quickly change direction.

2. Use both feet and all parts of the foot for this practice, performing different dribbling and turning techniques.

---

## Practice 4   Dribbling Team Game with Numbers    15 mins

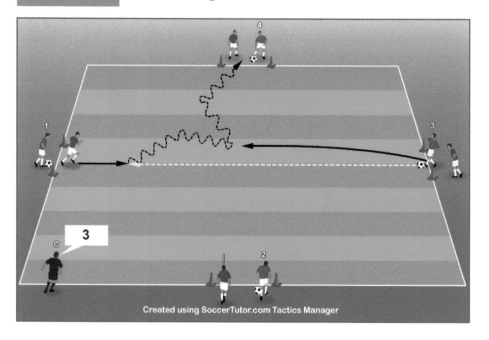

### Description

The players wait for the coach to call out a number which relates to a player.

Here, red no.3 passes the ball to a blue player and then moves towards them to become the defender.

The blue player who receives the ball tries to score in one of the other 3 goals by dribbling through the cones.

### Variation

If the goal is scored in the opposite goal it is worth double.

### Coaching Points

1. This exercise requires many different changes of directions and turns.
2. Use a directional first touch when receiving the pass to quickly dribble through one of the cone gates.

---

## Practice 5   5v5 with 6 Dribble Gates in a SSG    20-25 mins

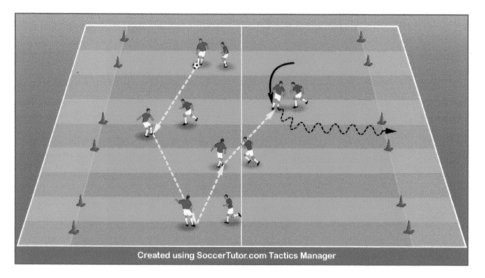

### Description

We play a 5v5 free game in an area 30 x 30 yards with 3 goals on each side.

The players must score a goal by dribbling through one of the cone gates.

### Variations

1. Tournament with more teams.
2. Stop the ball with the sole on the line to score.
3. Limit the touches.

## Practice 6   Free Small Sided Game    20 mins

**Primary Technical objective:** Running with the ball, feints/moves to beat and passing.

**Coordination Objective:** Quickness, adaptation, transformation and reactions.

**Secondary Technical Objective:** Changes of direction and shooting.

**Tactical Objective:** 1v1 play.

**Duration of Session:** 85-100 minutes

We recommend starting the session with exercises for general mobility to prevent injuries.

---

| Practice 1 | Dribble, Feint and Pass Practice | 10 mins |

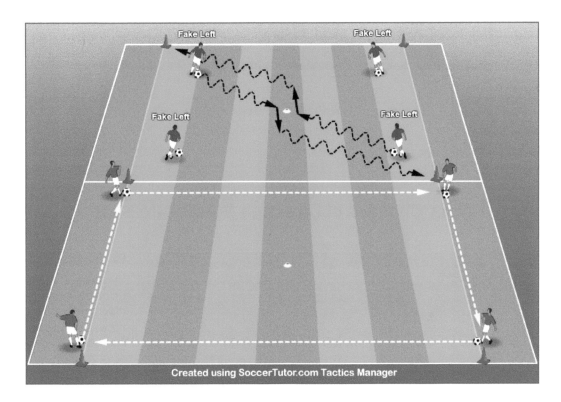

Created using SoccerTutor.com Tactics Manager

## Description

*STAGE 1*

4 players are at each corner of a square. The pair opposite to each other start dribbling and when they reach the centre, they make a feint to the left and go round the right side of the cone in the middle. They then dribble to the opposite position. The other 2 players do the same.

*STAGE 2*

When all 4 players have reached the opposite position, they pass the ball to each other in a clockwise direction using 1 or 2 touches.

## Variations

**1)** Use different type of feints determined by the coach. **2)** Follow your pass after passing (change positions).

## Coaching Point

1. When performing the feints they should do so as if beating a defender in a game, dropping their shoulder, bending their knees slightly and quickly changing direction.

---

## Practice 2   1v1 RWTB Race - 'Quickest Player Shoots'    5-10 mins

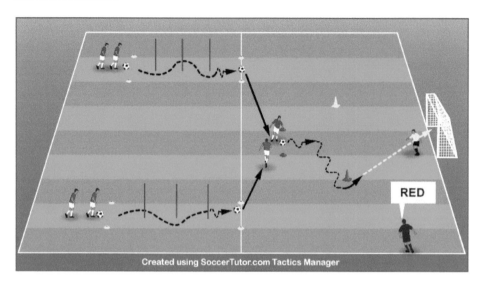

### Description

2 players start with a ball and dribble through the poles as shown and leave the ball in between the 2 cones.

The players race to the ball in the centre. The first one there aims to dribble the ball round one of the cones and score past the goalkeeper. The other player becomes the defender so we have a 1v1 situation.

The next 2 players start at the same time. There are 2 teams and the team with the most goals at the end wins.

### Variations

**1)** Play with the hands. **2)** Dribbling only with the right or left foot.

### Coaching Point

1. Although the players have to dribble the ball very quickly in this race, they need to still focus on accuracy through the poles using soft touches.

---

## Practice 3   Feints, Changes of Direction & Accurate Shot    15-20 mins

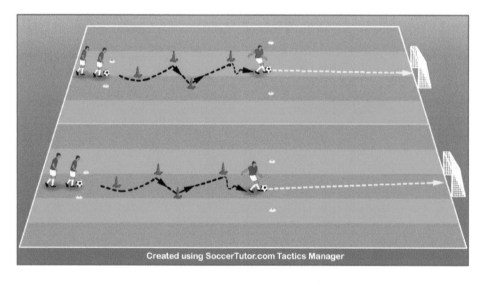

### Description

Players are in 2 groups dribbling as shown in the diagram, making various types of feints and then shooting in the small goals.

The second player begins as soon as the first one shoots.

This is a competition of which team can score the most goals.

### Variations

**1)** Free choice of feints. **2)** Assign specific feints e.g. scissors, double scissors, cut back, chop etc.

### Coaching Points

1. The feints should be performed at pace, as if moving away from a defender sharply in a game.

2. When assigning specific feints, demonstrate the correct execution if necessary.

---

## Practice 4    1v1 v Defender + 1v1 v Goalkeeper     15 mins

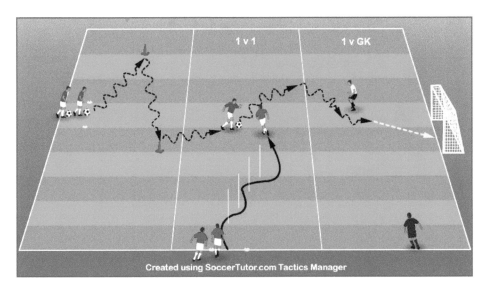

Created using SoccerTutor.com Tactics Manager

### Description

The red player starts by running through the poles.

The blue player dribbles and performs some feints and then takes the red player on in a 1v1, before trying to score past the goalkeeper.

If the red player wins the ball from the blue player, he can go into a 1v1 with the goalkeeper.

Change roles of the teams halfway through. The team with the most goals at the end wins.

### Variations

1. The goal counts double if a player does a feint specified by the coach.
2. The red players skip through the poles.

### Coaching Point

1. The player with the ball needs to use a change of pace or direction to quickly get into the 1 v GK zone and score.

---

## Practice 5    5v5 'Rugby Rules' Small Sided Game     20-25 mins

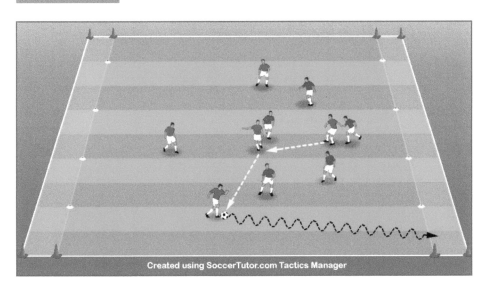

Created using SoccerTutor.com Tactics Manager

### Description

In an area 30 x 30 yards we play a 5v5 game.

The objective is to score by dribbling through the end zone.

Rugby rules are adopted, therefore the players are not allowed to pass the ball forward.

### Variations

1. Allow 1 forward pass.
2. If a goal is scored after a feint it is worth double.

---

## Practice 6    Free Small Sided Game     20 mins

---

# CHAPTER
## 4
# PASSING TRAINING UNIT

**Primary Technical objective:** Passing on the ground.

**Coordination Objective:** Quickness, adaptation, transformation and balance.

**Secondary Technical Objective:** Receiving and shooting.

**Tactical Objective:** Creating space, positioning and using width.

**Duration of Session:** 85-100 minutes

We recommend starting the session with exercises for general mobility to prevent injuries.

---

| Practice 1 | 'Psycho-Kinetics' Passing in Pairs Warm Up | 10 mins |

Created using SoccerTutor.com Tactics Manager

### Description

Players are in pairs and try to complete the highest possible number of passes in a preset time.

They must avoid the other pairs and show good awareness to be able to successfully pass to each other amongst all the 'traffic.'

The pair that complete the most passes in the allocated time win.

### Variations

**1)** Volley pass with the inside of foot **2)** Volley with instep. **3)** Headed pass. **4)** Receive the ball with the chest and volley pass with the inside of the foot.

### Coaching Points

1. Accuracy of pass, weight of pass and good communication are all key elements for this practice.
2. Players need to play with their heads up and have good awareness to avoid collisions and make successful passes to their teammate.
3. Close control is needed with directional first touches, especially when receiving with the chest.

---

## Practice 2  Skip, Pass, Receive, Dribble & Run Sequence   5-10 mins

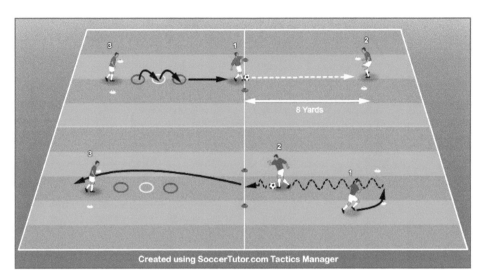

Created using SoccerTutor.com Tactics Manager

### Description

*PLAYER 1* hops through the rings with only the left foot and then passes to Player 2 with the right foot.

*PLAYER 2* receives the ball, dribbles the ball up to the cones and runs to the starting position where player 3 is waiting.

*PLAYER 3* starts the sequence again.

### Variation

Substitute the rings with a foam mat and ask the players to do a forward roll.

### Coaching Points

1. The pass should be weighted correctly to receive comfortably.
2. When receiving, the first touch should push the ball out of their feet to dribble forwards quickly.

## Practice 3  Accurate Passing in Pairs   15-20 mins

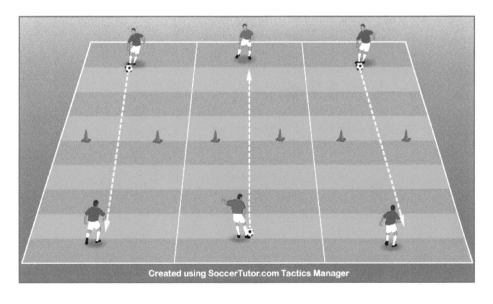

Created using SoccerTutor.com Tactics Manager

### Description

The players pass the ball to each other in pairs ensuring the ball is passed in between the cones.

The coach varies the part of the foot to be used:

1. The inside of the foot.
2. The instep.
3. The outside

### Variations

**1)** Volley pass with the inside of the foot. **2)** Half volley pass.

### Coaching Points

1. The accuracy and weight of pass needs to be correct.
2. In this simple drill, players should be able to aim for the inside or outside of a specific foot.

## Practice 4  Back to Goal 2v1 Dynamic Practice    20 mins

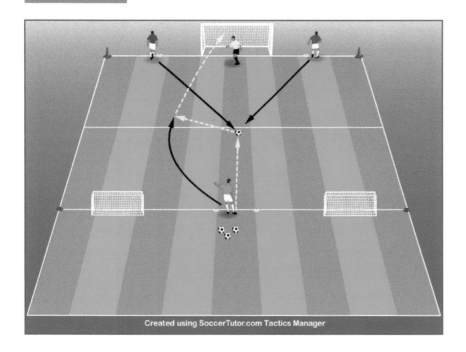

Created using SoccerTutor.com Tactics Manager

### Description

The orange player passes the ball into the middle with the inside of the foot.

The other players are turned away from the orange player.

When they hear the sound of the ball being passed they turn and run to the ball trying to play the ball back to the orange player.

Whoever arrives first to the ball plays with the orange player and they try to score in the big goal with the goalkeeper. If the defender wins the ball, they can score in one of the 2 smaller goals.

### Variations

1.  The orange player uses an aerial pass into the middle.
2.  Introduce the offside rule.

## Practice 5  Possession & Speed of Play in a SSG    20-25 mins

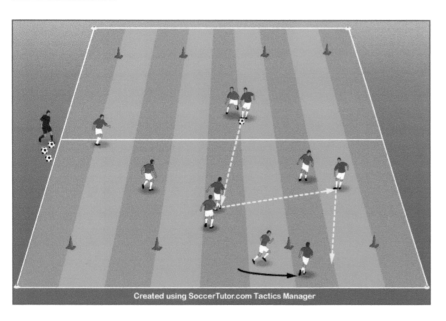

Created using SoccerTutor.com Tactics Manager

### Description

In an area 30 x 20 yards we have 4 goals made from cones 1.5 yards wide.

A goal is scored when a player passes the ball through the cones and a teammate receives the pass on the other side.

The ball can go through the goal both ways.

### Coaching Points

1.  There should be a mixture of passes to feet and passes into space.
2.  The timing of the movement with the pass is key to score 'goals' in this game.

## Practice 6  Free Small Sided Game    20 mins

**Primary Technical objective:** Passing on the ground.

**Coordination Objective:** Quickness and differentiation.

**Secondary Technical Objective:** Running with the ball.

**Tactical Objective:** Creating space, positioning and marking.

**Duration of Session:** 85-100 minutes

We recommend starting the session with exercises for general mobility to prevent injuries.

---

**Practice 1**   Accuracy & Weight of Pass - 'Aim for the Target'   **10 mins**

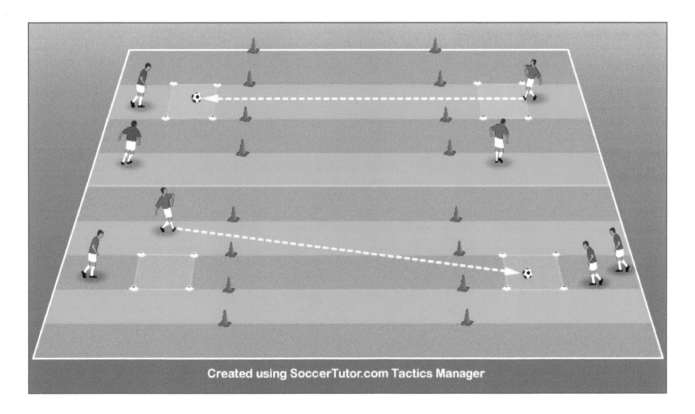

Created using SoccerTutor.com Tactics Manager

### Description

Players are in teams of 2 and must pass the ball through the cones that are set up and weight their pass so that it stops within the square (as shown in the diagram).

Every time the ball stops in the square the player gets a point for their team.

### Variations

1. Pass only with the weaker foot.
2. Pass with just the instep, the outside of the foot etc.

### Coaching Point

1. Use the part of the foot suitable for the distance and angle of the pass.

---

## Practice 2 — Accelerating & Changing Direction at Speed      5-10 mins

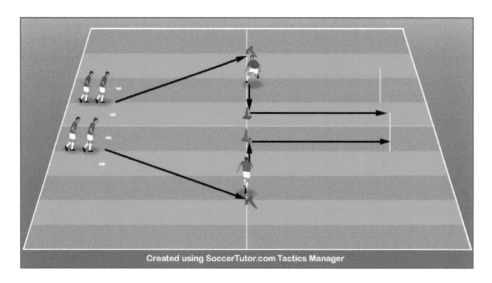

### Description

Players from each line sprint to the outside cones, knock them down, change direction and sprint to the inside cone (knocking that down to) and then change direction again to sprint inside through the poles.

The first player to go through the poles gets a point for their team.

### Variation

Knock the cones down with the hands.

### Coaching Point

1. This practice aims to train the movements needed to create space and receive when passing.

---

## Practice 3 — Pass, Move & Receive in a Square      15-20 mins

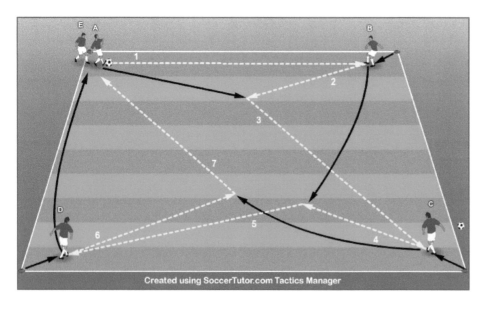

### Description

In a 10 x 10 yard square we have 5 players with 2 players in the starting position.

Player A passes to B who plays the ball back into A's path.

Player A passes to C who lays the ball back for B's run. B then passes to D who plays it into Player C's path to make the final pass back to the starting position.

All players move to the next position after their last pass (A to B, B to C, C to D and D to E. E starts the sequence again as Player A.

### Variations

1) Change the direction. 2) Execute the exercise with volleys starting with the ball in the hands.

### Coaching Points

1. The rhythm and timing of the movement together with the pass is key.
2. Players need to make sure their first touch is made on the move to maintain the fluency of the drill.

## Practice 4    Dynamic 2v2 Duel Games    20 mins

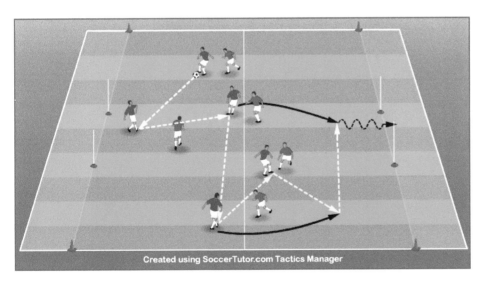

Exercise 1      Exercise 2

Created using SoccerTutor.com Tactics Manager

### Description

*EXERCISE 1*
Here we have a frontal 2v2 situation where the attackers try to score in the goal and the defenders try to win the ball (if they do they can dribble through the end zone to score).

*EXERCISE 2*
We again have a 2v2 but 1 defender starts from behind this time.

### Variations

**1)** Introduce the offside rule. **2)** Add 2 players outside the square to create a 4v2 numerical advantage.

### Coaching Points

1. Players should check away from their marker before moving to receive the ball.

2. The aim is to pass the ball forward quickly and score.

---

## Practice 5    5v5 Possession & Changing the Direction of Attack in a Small Sided Game    20-25 mins

Created using SoccerTutor.com Tactics Manager

### Description

Here we have a 5v5 small sided game.

The teams have to complete 5 passes before being allowed to score.

A goal is scored when a player dribbles through the poles.

### Variation

When the coach calls/ whistles, the players change the direction of attack and attack the opposite goal.

### Coaching Points

1. The players need to be aware and prepared to quickly change the direction of attack.

2. Encourage the players to communicate and be creative in their attacking combinations.

---

## Practice 6    Free Small Sided Game    20 mins

---

**Primary Technical objective:** Passing on the ground and 1-2 combinations.

**Coordination Objective:** Balance and motor reactions.

**Secondary Technical Objective:** Passing under pressure with possession play.

**Tactical Objective:** Creating space, positioning and pressing.

**Duration of Session:** 85-100 minutes

We recommend starting the session with exercises for general mobility to prevent injuries.

---

| Practice 1 | One-Two Combination, Pass & Follow | 10 mins |

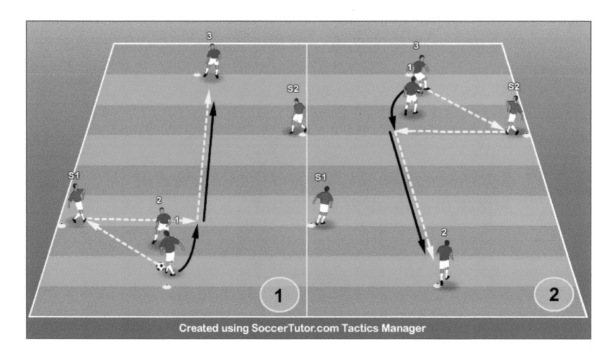

## Description

*STAGE 1*

Player 1 is under pressure from Player 2 and passes to S1 at the side, who passes the ball into the path of Player 1's run forward. When Player 1 receives the ball back, he passes to player 3 and then moves to apply pressure. Player 2 moves to Player 1's position.

*STAGE 2*

Player 3 receives the ball and starts the same sequence from the other end. He plays a 1-2 with S2 and then passes to Player 2 who then repeats Stage 1 under pressure from Player 3.

## Variations

1. Change the position of the side players to work on the other foot.

2. Play 1 touch elimination game for the player who misses the pass.

## Coaching Points

1. The weight of the 2nd pass is key so the teammate can run onto the ball without slowing down.

2. Progress from passive defender to a fully active defender.

---

## Practice 2 — 'Technique & Balance' Passing Exercise — 5-10 mins

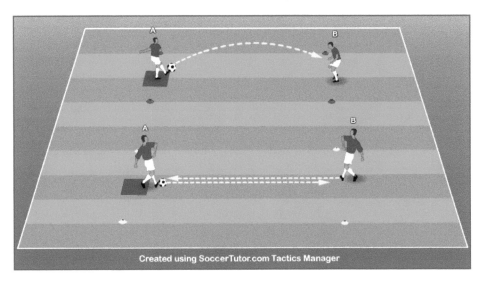

### Description

This exercise is performed in pairs. Player B throws/passes the ball to Player A who performs a series of passes (volley with inside of foot, volley with instep, receiving with the thigh and passing back etc) while standing on a balancing tool.

We recommend the players wear running shoes.

### Variation

Perform a series of 10 passes each.

### Coaching Points

1. Monitor the correct technique of the different passes - instep, volley etc.
2. The weight and accuracy of the first throw/pass is very important for the player on the balancing tool to be able to receive and pass back properly.

## Practice 3 — 'Give and Go' Passing Circle — 15-20 mins

### Description

6-7 players form a circle with 1 player in the middle.

Player A in the middle passes to player B and applies passive pressure.

Player B plays a 1-2 combination with player C. Player A moves into Player B's position.

Player B then makes the next pass and applies pressure as the sequence continues.

### Coaching Points

1. Make sure the players communicate and heads are up.
2. Start the drill with 2 touches and quickly progress to 1 touch to speed up play.

## Practice 4   One-Two Combinations in a 2v1 Duel

### 20 mins

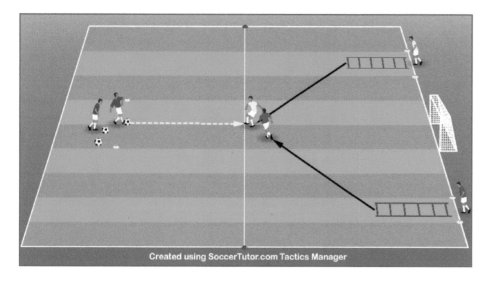

Created using SoccerTutor.com Tactics Manager

### Description

The players are split into teams and the blue player passes the ball into the middle. The yellow and red players run through the ladder and then they sprint towards the ball. The first player to the ball passes back to the blue player and we have a 2v1 game.

2 points if the goal is scored with a 1-2 combination.

### Variations

**1)** Substitute the rings with poles or a forward roll. **2)** Allow the defender to be able to score a goal too.

### Coaching Points

1. Players need quick steps lifting the knees when running through the ladder.

2. The correct body shape when receiving is important, making sure to shield the ball from the defender.

## Practice 5   'Give and Go' 3 Team Possession Game

### 20-25 mins

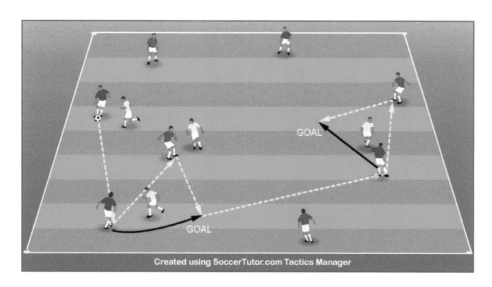

GOAL

GOAL

Created using SoccerTutor.com Tactics Manager

### Description

2 teams (blue and red) play against 1 team (yellow).

A goal is scored every time a 1-2 combination is completed.

The yellow (defending) team try to win the ball.

Change the defending team every 2 minutes.

### Variation

The 1-2 combination has to be between different colours.

### Coaching Points

1. With 1-2 combinations, the second pass needs to be out in front of the player to run onto.

2. Good positioning and body shape help to be able to pass the ball first time.

## Practice 6   Free Small Sided Game

### 20 mins

**Primary Technical objective:** Penetrating passes.

**Coordination Objective:** Quickness and balance.

**Secondary Technical Objective:** Receiving the ball and shooting with accuracy.

**Tactical Objective:** Creating space, positioning and pressing.

**Duration of Session:** 85-100 minutes

We recommend starting the session with exercises for general mobility to prevent injuries.

---

**Practice 1** **4v2 Possession - Passing, Receiving & Speed of Play 10 mins**

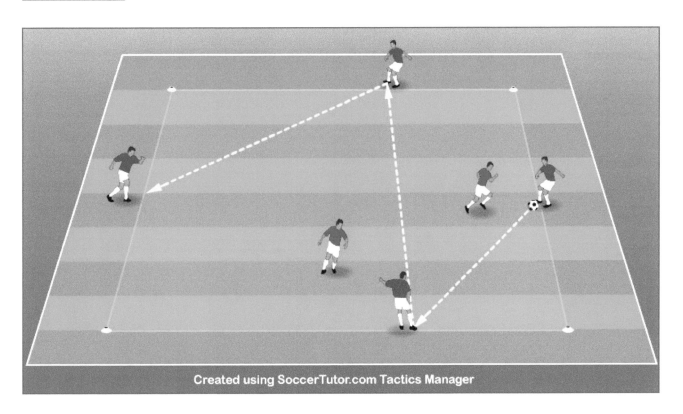

Created using SoccerTutor.com Tactics Manager

### Description

We play 4v2 for this possession game. The blue players are on the outside of the square and try to complete 10 passes to win 1 point. The passes must be on the ground.

The red players act as defenders and can move freely inside the square. They try to block/intercept the ball before the blue team gets to 10 passes.

Change roles halfway through. The team with the most points win.

### Variation

Play with only 2 touches and give 1 point every time the ball is passed in between the 2 defenders.

### Coaching Points

1. The player in possession should always have 2 options so the players need to move to create good angles.

2. The 2 red defenders must press together to close the passing angles making it harder to keep possession.

---

## Practice 2 — Sprinting & Agility with a Goalkeeper — 5-10 mins

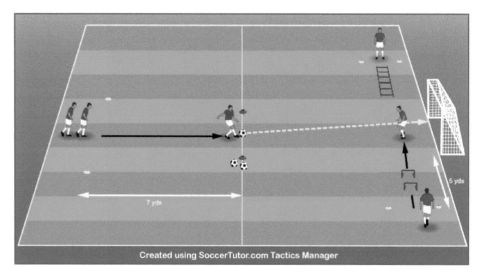

**Description**

The red player sprints to the ball placed in the middle of the cones and shoots at goal.

The blue player starts by jumping over 2 hurdles or through a speed ladder and then running to become the goalkeeper.

**Variation**

A goal is worth 2 points if the player scores in the half of the goal called out by the coach (left or right side).

**Coaching Point**

1. This drill is used to practice forward runs which lead to a shot and we introduce a pass in the next drill.

---

## Practice 3 — Ball Control, Passing & Agility with Shooting — 15-20 mins

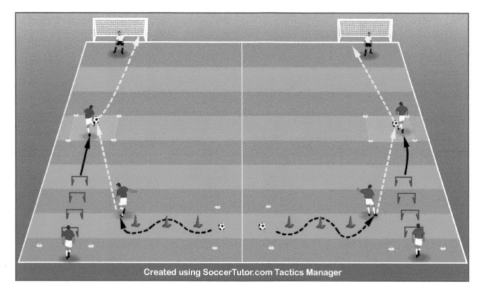

**Description**

The first player dribbles the ball around the cones and passes the ball into the square for their teammate.

The other player has jumped over the 4 hurdles and sprints into the square to receive the pass and shoot at goal.

The team that scores the most goals wins the game.

**Coaching Points**

1. The pass from player A and the run from player B must be done at maximum speed.

2. The pass should be accurate and weighted correctly to be out in front of the player who can run onto the ball and shoot quickly.

## Practice 4 — Passing Combinations with a 3v2 Advantage — 20 mins

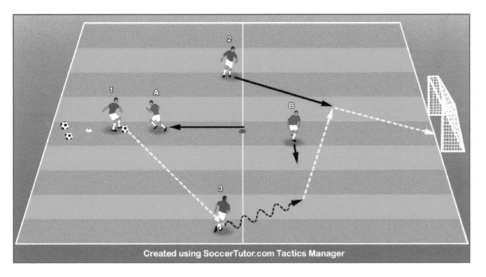

Created using SoccerTutor.com Tactics Manager

### Description

Player 1 starts with the ball and as player A applies pressure he makes a pass to player 2 or 3 based on which opponent player B marks.

Player 1 must use the inside of his left foot to pass to player 3 and the inside of his right foot to pass to player 2.

Player B's starting position is behind player A and the blues have a 3v2 situation with the aim to score in the goal.

Change defenders often.

### Variation

Pass with the the outside of the foot.

### Coaching Points

1. Awareness is needed to choose which side to pass to.
2. Move the ball quickly to exploit the numerical advantage.

## Practice 5 — 7v7 Possession Game with Target Players — 20-25 mins

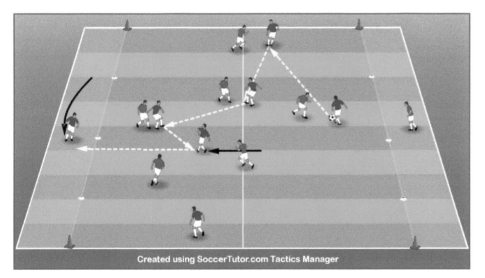

Created using SoccerTutor.com Tactics Manager

### Description

In an area 40 x 30 yards, 2 teams of 7 players play a game with a target player at each end in a 5 yard zone.

The objective is to make a penetrating pass to the target player after completing 5 passes.

### Variations

1. A point is won if the target player can pass the ball back to another player after receiving in the end zone.
2. The pass to the target player has to be a lob and he must control the ball in the air.

### Coaching Points

1. Correct body shape (open up on the half turn) and positioning is important to view where the next pass goes.
2. Using the full width by switching the play maximises the space and makes it easier to maintain possession.

## Practice 6 — Free Small Sided Game — 20 mins

**Primary Technical objective:** Passing on the ground, 1-2 combinations and 'pass and follow.'

**Coordination Objective:** Quickness, balance and motor combinations.

**Secondary Technical Objective:** Directional receiving of the ball and shooting.

**Tactical Objective:** Creating space, positioning, overlapping and counter attacking.

**Duration of Session:** 85-100 minutes

We recommend starting the session with exercises for general mobility to prevent injuries.

---

| Practice 1 | Passing and Shooting Challenge - 'How Many?' | 10 mins |

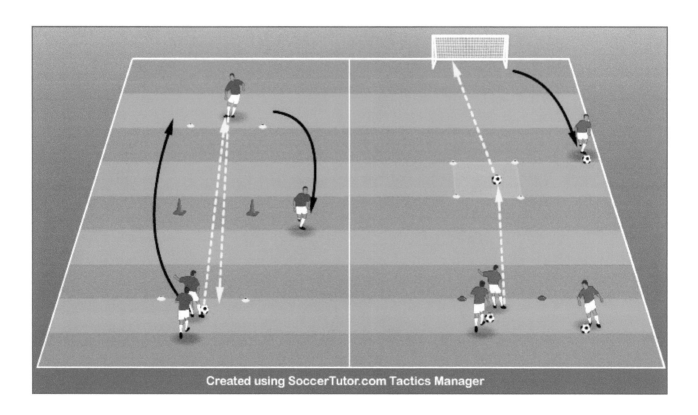

Created using SoccerTutor.com Tactics Manager

## Description

The blue team must complete a predetermined number of passes through the cones. After they pass, they run to the other end to receive another pass.

At the same time, the red team must score as many goals as they possible can. The players pass the ball to themselves in the square, run forward and shoot.

## Variations

1. The blue team passes the ball with a volley or half volley out of their hands.
2. The red team dribble and shoot.

## Coaching Points

1. Both groups need to play at a high tempo (1 touch passing and shooting).
2. The weight and accuracy of pass need to be correct to keep the flow of this drill going.

---

## Practice 2   Coordination and Passing Relay

### 5-10 mins

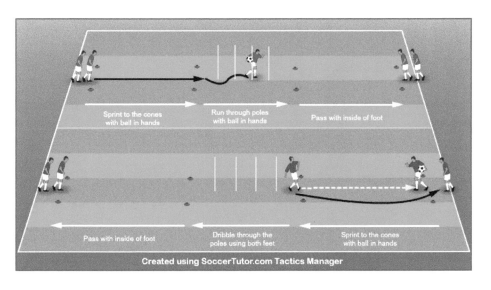

Sprint to the cones with ball in hands

Run through poles with ball in hands

Pass with inside of foot

Pass with inside of foot

Dribble through the poles using both feet

Sprint to the cones with ball in hands

Created using SoccerTutor.com Tactics Manager

**Description**

The first player in each line runs up to the the poles and through them with the ball in their hands. At the end, they pass the ball on the ground to the next player waiting on the opposite side.

The player that receives the ball, picks it up runs to the poles and dribbles the ball through them before passing to the player waiting on the other side.

The team that completes the most passes in a predetermined time win the game.

**Variation**

Volley with the inside of the foot, the instep or half volley.

**Coaching Points**

1. This practice should be done at full speed.

2. The players need good rhythm in the transitions to different parts of the drill.

## Practice 3   Pass, Receive and Follow in a Square

### 15-20 mins

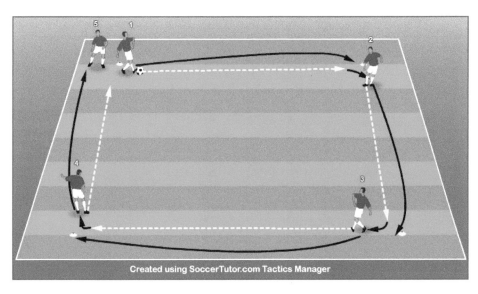

Created using SoccerTutor.com Tactics Manager

**Description**

Player 1 passes to 2 and takes his position.

Player 2 passes to 3, 3 to 4 and finally 4 to 5. Player 5 becomes Player 1 and starts the sequence again.

Players follow every pass to take up the next position.

They receive with the left foot and pass with the right.

**Variation**

Change the direction and which foot they receive/pass with.

**Coaching Points**

1. The players need to make sure their first touch is made on the move to maintain the fluency of this drill.

2. Make sure the players communicate with their teammates and heads are up.

## Practice 4 — 2v1 Combination Play with Overlapping Run — 20 mins

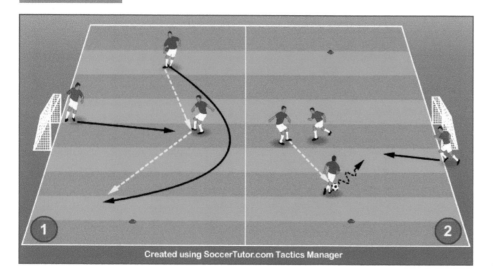

Created using SoccerTutor.com Tactics Manager

### Description
We have a 2v1 game in an area 20 x 15 yards.

*STAGE 1*
The player who starts with the ball must make a pass and create space with an overlapping run to receive back (with the aim to score).

*STAGE 2*
Here we have the same scenario, but once the first defender has been beaten, another defender will enter for a new 2v1. The aim for the attackers is still to score in the goal.

### Variation
Players pass then make a diagonal cutting run instead of an overlap.

### Coaching Points
1. The overlapping run should start as soon as the first player plays the pass.
2. Pass should be weighted perfectly for the overlapping run (in front of them)

## Practice 5 — 5v5 End to End Possession Game — 20-25 mins

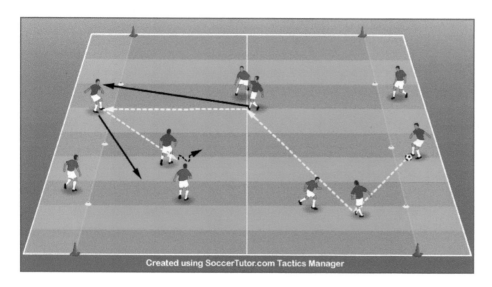

Created using SoccerTutor.com Tactics Manager

### Description
We have a 5v5 in an area 40 x 25 yards. 2 players from each team stand in the end zones (1 at each end).

A point is scored every time the ball is worked from 1 target player to the other.

When a pass is made to the target player, this player enters the middle area and the passing player takes his place. The team maintains possession to attack in the opposite direction.

### Coaching Points
1. Correct body shape (open up on the half-turn) and positioning is important to view the options for where the next pass is going.
2. When the players are exchanging positions in the end zones, they need to do so quickly and provide a passing option to keep possession.

## Practice 6 — Free Small Sided Game — 20 mins

**Primary Technical objective:** Passing in the air.

**Coordination Objective:** Quickness, dynamic balance and reading the path of the ball.

**Secondary Technical Objective:** Receiving the ball in the air.

**Tactical Objective:** Creating space and quick counter attacking.

**Duration of Session:** 85-100 minutes

We recommend starting the session with exercises for general mobility to prevent injuries.

---

**Practice 1**  Receiving, Juggling and Passing Warm Up    10 mins

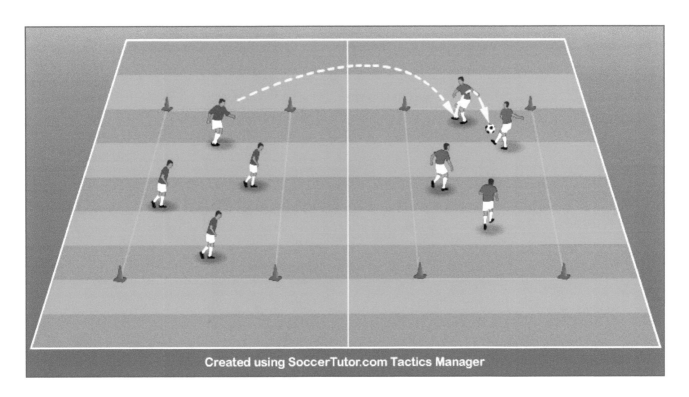

*Created using SoccerTutor.com Tactics Manager*

### Description

4 players are in each 10 x 10 yard square and must throw the ball into the opposite square. The game starts with a blue player throwing the ball using the throw-in technique. Progress to aerial passing with feet.

The team receiving the ball try to keep it up for as long as possible by juggling between the 4 players (3 touches maximum each). Count how many they manage. Once the ball hits the floor, the reds then throw the ball into the blue team's square and they do the same.

### Coaching Points

1. The players should try to use all parts of the foot, thigh, chest and head to maximise control of the ball.

2. The aim here is to pass between the 2 boxes and not to score points. The passes should be hit high in the air for their teammates to control.

## Practice 2   Roll, Run, Volley Pass and Sprint     5-10 mins

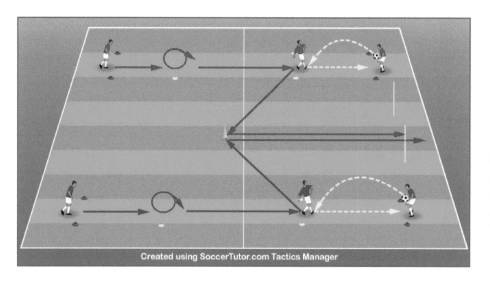

**Description**

Players are divided into 2 teams. The first player does a forward roll and runs to control the ball in the air thrown by a teammate and passes it back to him.

After controlling the ball, they run to touch the cone in the middle and sprint though the poles. The firstplayer to cross the line wins a point for their team.

### Variations

**1)** Pass the ball with a header. **2)** Volley pass using the inside of the foot. **3)** Control with the chest and pass.

### Coaching Points

1. Players should be at full speed and change direction by slowing down while slightly bending their knees.

2. The accuracy and technique of the throw and the pass should be monitored.

## Practice 3   Pass, Receive in the Air, Dribble and Shoot     15-20 mins

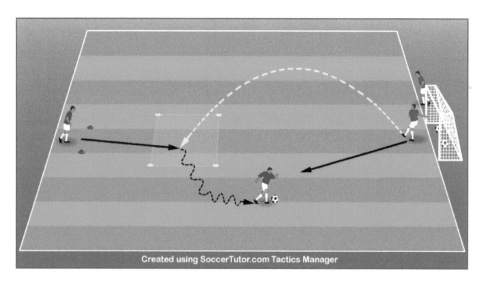

**Description**

The red player volleys the ball into the box.

The blue player starts 5 yards outside the box, runs into it and receives, directing the ball with his first touch outside of the box (left, right or forward) and shoots in the goal.

### Variation

The ball is lobbed high and the player must control the ball within the box before dribbling and shooting.

### Coaching Points

1. The players should take a directional first touch out of the square to move forward and dribble.

2. The players should try to use all parts of the foot, thigh, chest and head to maximise control of the ball.

## Practice 4    Lofted Passes into the End Zones in a SSG    20-25 mins

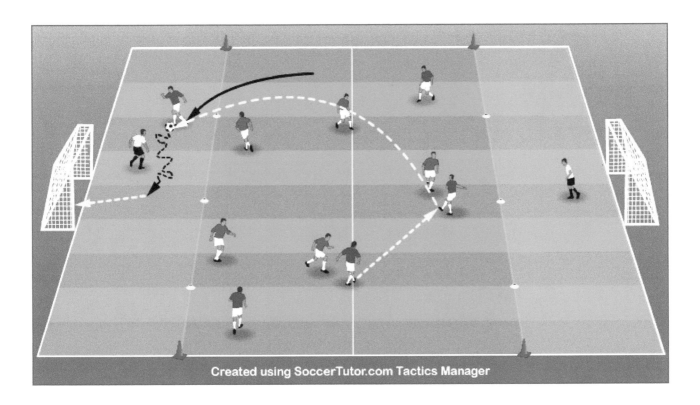

Created using SoccerTutor.com Tactics Manager

### Description

2 teams play in an area 40 x 30 yards. No defenders are allowed in the end zones.

The attacking players can run into the end zone to receive a pass in the air, control the ball and shoot past the goalkeeper.

This is only allowed if the pass is played in the air and the player receives the ball before it bounces.

### Variation

The final pass into the end zone is only allowed after 5 completed passes.

## Practice 5    Free Small Sided Game      20 mins

**Primary Technical objective:** Passing in the air.

**Coordination Objective:** Quickness, dynamic balance and reading the path of the ball.

**Secondary Technical Objective:** Receiving the ball and 1 touch passing.

**Tactical Objective:** Creating space, quick counter attacking and positioning.

**Duration of Session:** 85-100 minutes

We recommend starting the session with exercises for general mobility to prevent injuries.

---

## Practice 1    Football Tennis Game                    10 mins

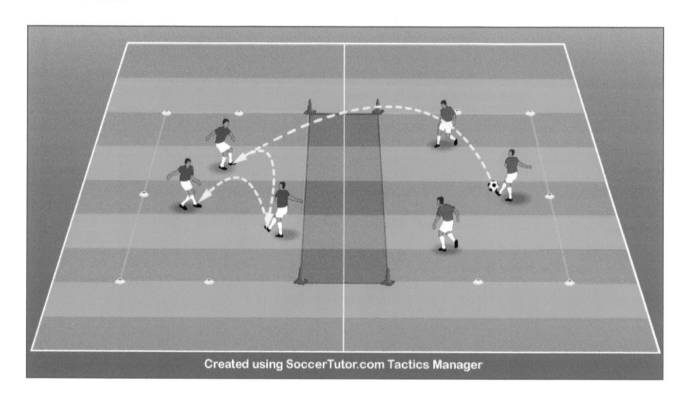

Created using SoccerTutor.com Tactics Manager

### Description

This is a game with tennis rules. We play with a maximum of 3 touches and only 1 bounce. At least 1 pass to a teammate is needed before playing the ball back over to the other side.

If you do not have a football tennis net, the net can be represented by the four traffic cones as shown in the diagram.

### Variation

Limit the players to 1 touch and 3 passes needed before playing the ball back over.

### Coaching Points

1. The players should try to use all parts of the foot, thigh, chest and head to maximise control of the ball.

2. The aim here is to pass between the 2 boxes and the passes should be hit high in the air for the other team to control.

---

## Practice 2 — Jump, 1-2, Change Direction and Shoot — 5-10 mins

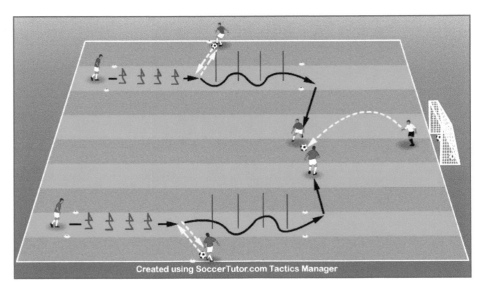

*Created using SoccerTutor.com Tactics Manager*

### Description

Players jump over the hurdles, then stop.

A teammate on the side throws/passes the ball for the player to volley or pass back with the inside of the foot.

The player then runs through the poles and sprints to the ball thrown up in the air by the goalkeeper, to play a 1v1 with the opponent.

### Variation

The first player to receive the ball from the goalkeeper can shoot unopposed.

### Coaching Point

1. The throw/pass for the 1-2 combination should be in front of the player so they can pass the ball back while on the move, to prevent slowing down in this competitive race.

---

## Practice 3 — Quick Reactions & Speed of Play in a 2v1 Duel Game — 20 mins

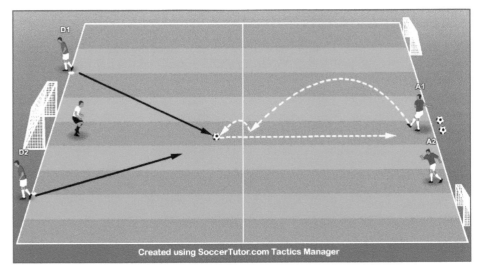

*Created using SoccerTutor.com Tactics Manager*

### Description

The blue player chips the ball into the middle of the field. The red players stand with their backs to play.

At the sound of the ball being kicked they turn and sprint to the ball. The first player to the ball passes it back to the blue player and a 2v1 situation is created (A1 & A2 v D1 in the diagram).

If the defender wins the ball he can score in either of the 2 mini goals.

### Variations

1. Players competing for the ball must perform a coordination exercise before sprinting to the ball.
2. Play with the offside rule.

### Coaching Point

1. To utilise the numerical advantage, the player with the ball should wait for the defender to commit themselves and then pass into space to their teammate.

---

**Practice 4**  **4v3 Numerical Advantage in a 3 Zone SSG**  **20-25 mins**

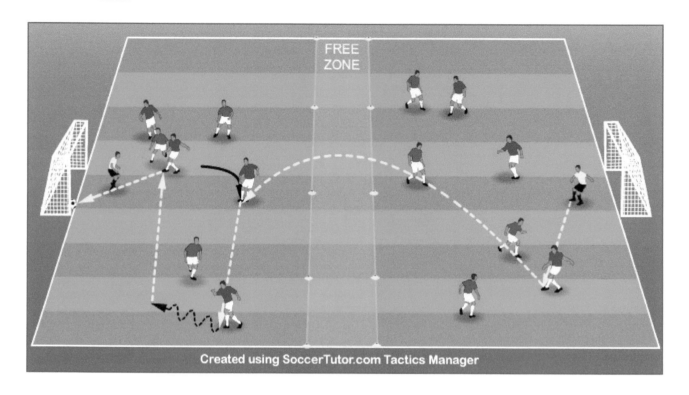

Created using SoccerTutor.com Tactics Manager

### Description

2 teams play 8v8 in an area 40 x 30 yards. In the centre there is a free zone which is 7 yards wide. We have 1 zone at either side and in each zone there are 4 attackers playing against 3 defenders.

The drill starts with a pass from the goalkeeper to the defenders and the attackers can only apply passive pressure. The defenders play aerial passes to the attackers that play with a 4v3 numerical advantage.

If the attackers score a goal, the play starts again with the opposition's goalkeeper. If the defenders intercept the ball they must play the ball to their attackers in the other zone.

Only 1 player at a time can enter the free zone. The player's team must have possession of the ball in the other half if he is to enter the free zone (where you are free and unmarked). When an attacker receives the ball in the free zone, they aim to beat a defender and shoot on goal.

### Variation

Play the game with equal numbers in both zones (e.g 3v3, 4v4).

### Coaching Points

1. The defenders need to move the ball to the other zone quickly as they have a numerical disadvantage.
2. Players need to check away from their marker before moving to receive the ball, especially when receiving from the other zone (to create space).

---

**Practice 5**  **Free Small Sided Game**  **20 mins**

---

**Primary Technical objective:** Passing in the air.

**Coordination Objective:** Quickness, motor reactions and reading the ball's trajectory.

**Secondary Technical Objective:** Receiving the ball, 1 touch passes and shooting.

**Tactical Objective:** Creating space and positioning.

**Duration of Session:** 85-100 minutes

We recommend starting the session with exercises for general mobility to prevent injuries.

| Practice 1 | **Juggling in Pairs Over a Net** | **10 mins** |

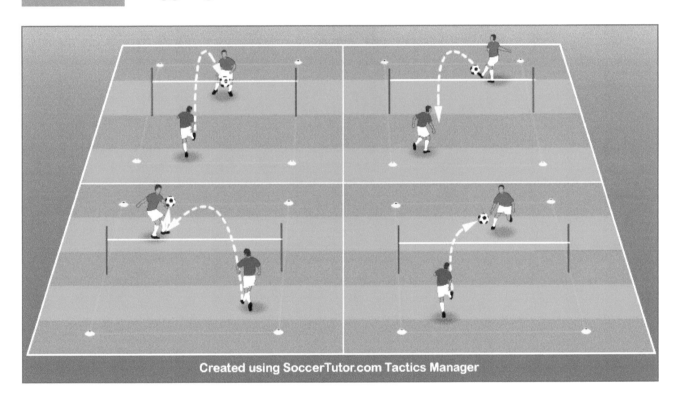

Created using SoccerTutor.com Tactics Manager

### Description

2 players juggle the ball and pass it to each other over the net. Allow free play to begin with before applying rules and specific combinations.

Poles with string (as shown in the diagram) also work perfectly for this practice.

### Variations

1. Play with exactly 3 touches.
2. Allow 1 bounce.
3. Players can only use their heads.
4. Use half volleys, making first time passes.

### Coaching Points

1. Monitor the correct technique for receiving and passing the ball in the air.
2. Make sure players use their instep and the inside of their foot to volley pass in this exercise.

## Practice 2 — Quick Reactions, Turning and 1st Time Shot — 5-10 mins

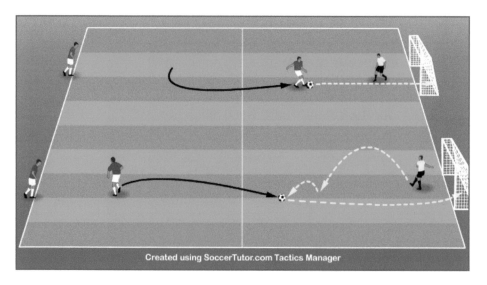

Created using SoccerTutor.com Tactics Manager

### Description

Players start with their backs facing the goal and when they hear the goalkeeper kick the ball they quickly turn around, move to the ball and shoot first time.

2 players go at the same time and a point is won for the player who scores first.

### Variation

Players turn and perform a forward roll before shooting.

### Coaching Points

1. Players need to judge the flight of the ball to adjust their body and be able to strike first time.
2. When striking the head should be over the ball with the back straight.

---

## Practice 3 — Passing and Receiving with Good Communication — 20 mins

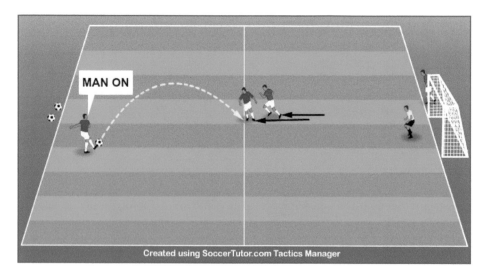

MAN ON

Created using SoccerTutor.com Tactics Manager

### Description

The blue player passes the ball in the air to his teammate and depending on the defenders positioning, calls "man on" and receives the ball back.

We then have a 2v1 situation with the aim to score.

Alternatively, he can call "turn" then a frontal 2v1 situation is created.

### Variations

1. Introduce the offside rule.
2. The player passes the ball back with the head.

### Coaching Points

1. The player needs to use their body as a barrier between the ball and the defender (shielding).
2. In a 2v1 situation, the player with the ball can wait for the defender to commit, then pass into the space.

---

## Practice 4 — Support Play with Target Players in a SSG    20-25 mins

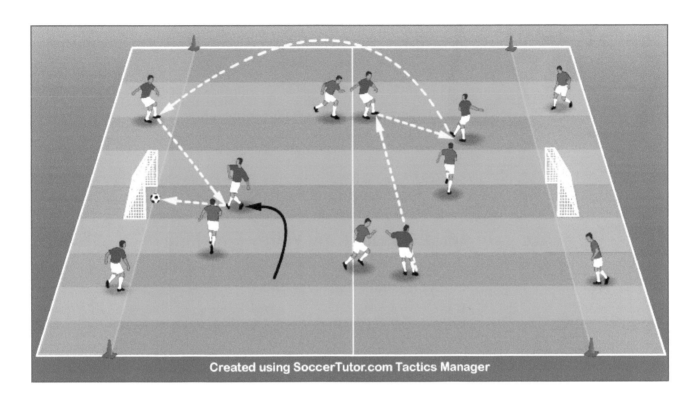

Created using SoccerTutor.com Tactics Manager

### Description

2 teams play 6v6 in an area 40 x 30 yards with 2 target players from each team standing either side of the goal they are attacking.

A goal can only be scored after an aerial pass to a target player, who must then knock the ball back first time for a teammate to shoot on goal.

---

### Practice 5    Free Small Sided Game    20 mins

---

**Primary Technical objective:** Passing in the air and crossing.

**Coordination Objective:** Dynamic balance and reading the ball's trajectory.

**Secondary Technical Objective:** Directional receiving of the ball, dribbling, acrobatics and shooting.

**Tactical Objective:** Quick counter attacking and positioning.

**Duration of Session:** 85-100 minutes

---

We recommend starting the session with exercises for general mobility to prevent injuries.

---

### Practice 1   Accurate Aerial Passing and Volley Finishing        10 mins

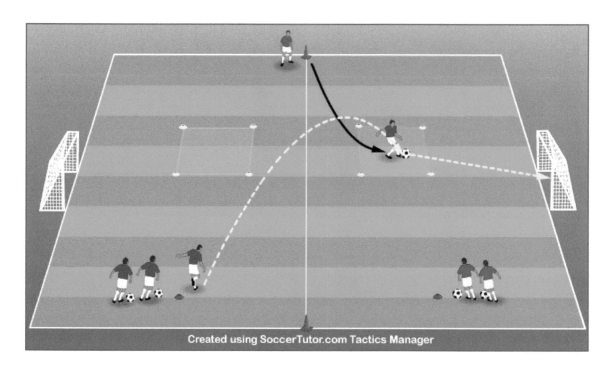

Created using SoccerTutor.com Tactics Manager

### Description

2 teams have a competition with the aim of scoring the most goals. 1 player from each team (the attackers) are in position on one side. The rest of the players have a ball each on the other side (as shown).

The aim is to play an aerial pass which must land in the square for the oncoming teammate on the other side to volley into the goal. The player that made the pass then moves to become an attacker and take their turn to shoot. The attacker joins the queue to pass.

After 3 goes each, the players switch sides so they practice reading the balls trajectory from the left and the right.

### Variation

Receive the ball in the air with the first touch and then volley the ball into the goal with the second.

### Coaching Points

1. Demonstrate the proper technique for striking a volley.

2. Players need to keep their eyes fixed on the flight of the ball, watching it all the way to their foot.

3. The chip passes need to be accurate and played in front of the player to run onto and strike.

---

## Practice 2 — Pass, Receive and Quickly Dribble

**5-10 mins**

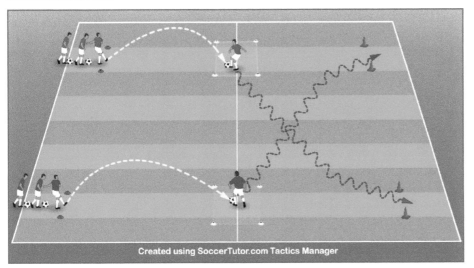

Created using SoccerTutor.com Tactics Manager

### Description

The first player chips the ball into the square where the player is positioned.

The player in the square controls the ball, then quickly dribble towards the opposite goal (as shown).

The first player to dribble through the cones wins a point for their team.

### Variation

This exercise can also be done with a pass on the ground.

### Coaching Points

1. Players should take a directional first touch towards their end destination to maximise their speed.

2. The pass needs to be accurate and aimed to the correct foot to make the transition to dribbling easier.

---

## Practice 3 — 3v3 (+2) Crossing & Finishing with Side Zones

**20 mins**

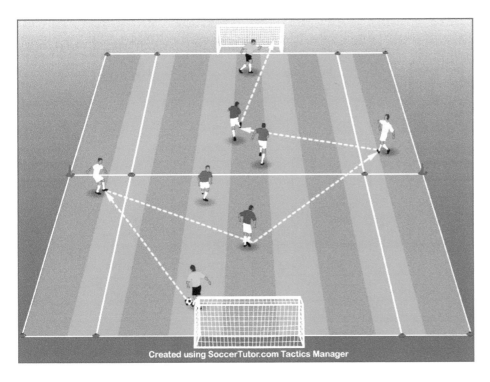

Created using SoccerTutor.com Tactics Manager

### Description

In an area 20 x 15 yards a game of 2v2 + goalkeepers is played with 2 neutral support players on the outside who play with the team in possession.

If a goal is scored from a cross from one of the outside players, the goal counts double.

### Variations

1. The outside player is limited to 2 touches.

2. A goal from an acrobatic shot is worth 3 points (overhead kick, scissor kick etc).

---

## Practice 4 — Passing & Support Play with Overlapping Runs in a 7v7 Small Sided Game

**20-25 mins**

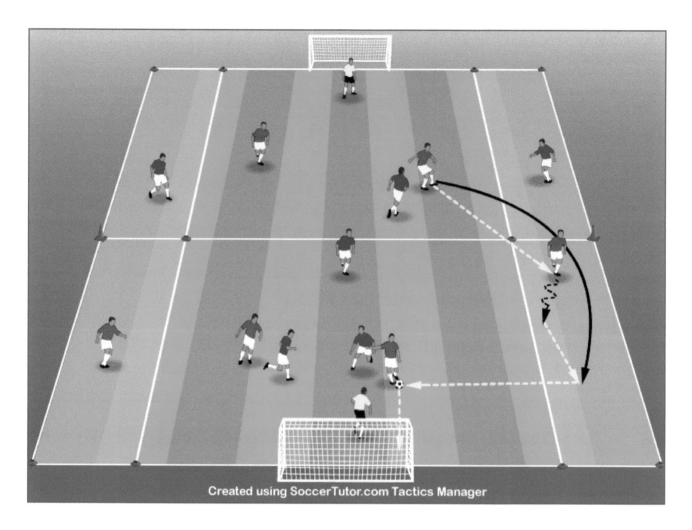

Created using SoccerTutor.com Tactics Manager

### Description

In an area 40 x 30 yards, we play 7v7 with 2 players from each team in each of the 2 outside channels/zones.

A goal can only be scored after an overlapping run by a player from the main area (as shown in the diagram).

The player who makes the overlap then switches positions with the player in the side zone.

### Variation

The opposition player in the outside channel can defend actively to create a 2v1 situation.

### Coaching Points

1. The wide player should dribble inside to create space for the overlapping run.
2. The pass should be out in front of the player to run onto, allowing them to cross the ball with 1 touch.

---

**Practice 5   Free Small Sided Game**  **20 mins**

---

**Primary Technical objective:** Passing in the air and crossing.

**Coordination Objective:** Reading the trajectory of the ball, dynamic balance, motor reactions and quickness.

**Secondary Technical Objective:** Receiving and directional control.

**Tactical Objective:** Marking, creating space and overlapping.

**Duration of Session:** 85-100 minutes

We recommend starting the session with exercises for general mobility to prevent injuries.

## Practice 1 — Low Crosses (Passes) Across the Box and Finishing 10 mins

Created using SoccerTutor.com Tactics Manager

### Description

The outside players receive the first pass and then dribble the ball towards the touchline and cross the ball for their 2 teammates that try to score. Practice from both sides. Change the player's roles often.

This can be a team game and the team that scores the most goals win the game.

### Variations

1. Pass the ball forward and then run onto it and cross (instead of dribbling).
2. Cross when the ball is stationary.

### Coaching Points

1. The pass and the run need to be timed well together to prevent the player having to slow down or halt their run before shooting at goal.
2. The pass out wide should be in front of the player on the flank to run onto without breaking stride.

## Practice 2    Pass, Dribble and Press with Quick Reactions    5-10 mins

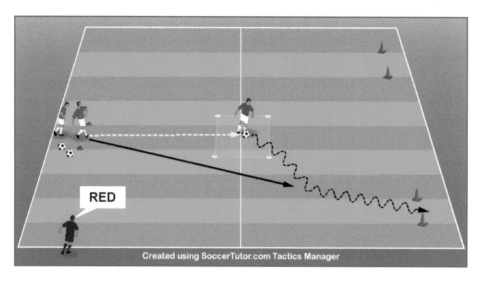

### Description

The red player passes the ball into the square. The blue player controls the ball and dribbles it through the cones that the coach calls out (red in diagram).

The red player who passed the ball becomes the defender and the blue player must dribble through the cones before the red player can intercept the ball.

### Variation

The pass from the red player can be a throw-in.

### Coaching Points

1. Receive the pass with an open body shape on the half turn.

2. The player receiving needs to be alert to react to whatever colour the coach calls out.

## Practice 3    Passing and Receiving - 'Moving Target Practice'    20 mins

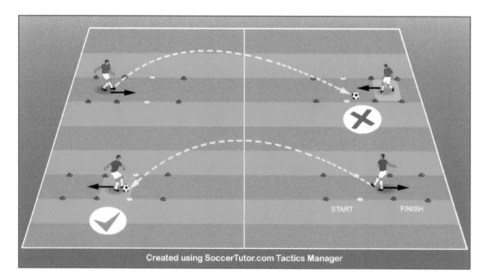

### Description

Players stand as shown in the diagram and there are 3 zones. The starting position can either be in the front or back zone.

Players pass the ball to each other in the air. A successful pass has to be controlled within the zone.

After each successful pass, the player moves position along the cones into the next zone.

The team that have both players receive successfully in the 'Finish Zone' first get a point.

### Variations

1. Receive and pass with the same foot.

2. Receive and pass with both feet.

3. Receiving with the chest.

## Practice 4 — 2v1 Play on the Flank and in the Penalty Area — 20 mins

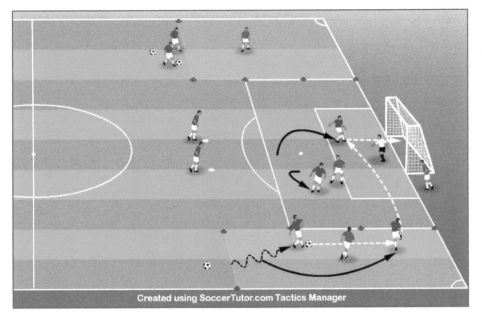

Created using SoccerTutor.com Tactics Manager

### Description

2 situations of 2v1 are created.

On the flank, players have a 2v1 with the aim to cross the ball.

In the other situation, 2 attackers play against 1 defender who must choose who to mark before the cross is taken.

The crosser should try to pass the ball to the player that is not marked.

### Variations

1. 2v1 on the flank with an overlapping run.

2. Introduce another defender to create a 2v2 situation in the penalty area.

## Practice 5 — Passing, Crossing & Finishing in a 7v7 SSG — 20-25 mins

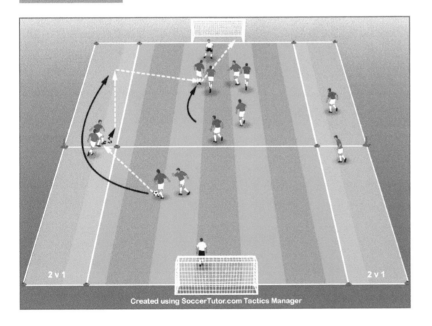

2 v 1

2 v 1

Created using SoccerTutor.com Tactics Manager

### Description

2 players of each team are positioned in the outside channel/zone.

These players in these side zones cannot be challenged and can freely cross the ball.

A goal directly from one of their crosses is worth 3 points.

### Variations

1. The player that passes the ball to the outside player runs into the channel and makes an overlapping run to receive the pass and cross the ball (as in diagram).

2. The player that passes the ball enters the channel to create a 2v1 against the opponent who is now active.

## Practice 6 — Free Small Sided Game — 20 mins

# CHAPTER

## 5

# Shooting Training Unit

**Primary Technical objective:** Shooting.

**Coordination Objective:** Balancing on one foot and flexibility of the kicking foot.

**Secondary Technical Objective:** One- two combinations and shooting with the weaker foot.

**Tactical Objective:** Creating space, positioning and pressing.

**Duration of Session:** 85-100 minutes

We recommend starting the session with exercises for general mobility to prevent injuries.

---

| Practice 1 | Shooting Practice with 1-2 Combination | 10 mins |

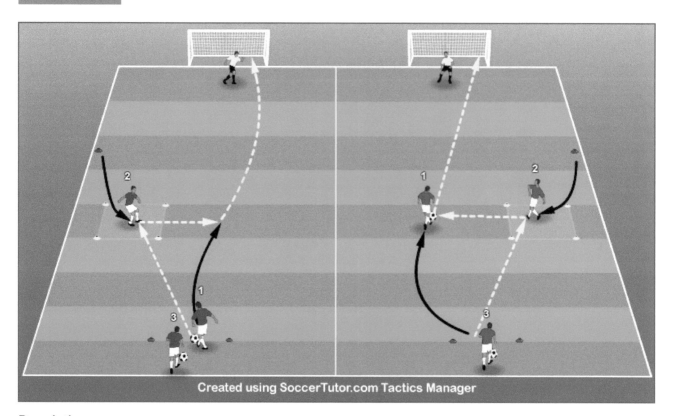

Created using SoccerTutor.com Tactics Manager

### Description

2 teams compete in a game where the player must score a goal after a 1-2 combination with a teammate.

Player 1 passes the ball into the square where player 2 has dropped back to receive. Player 2 uses 1 touch to pass the ball into the path of player 1's forward run. Player 1 shoots at goal.

The team that score the most goals win. Run the drill from the left and right side.

### Variations

1. Pass the ball in the air into the square and catch with the hands before volleying the ball.
2. Change the angle/direction of the movement of the player who passes from the square.

### Coaching Points

1. The accuracy and weight of the pass needs to be correct.
2. The rhythm and timing of the movement together with the pass is key.

---

## Practice 2 — Balance, Mobility and Flexibility for Shooting     10 mins

**Description**

Keeping balance on top of a block, the players first swing their legs sideways one at a time, and then do the same with a straight kick.

We work on the flexibility of the hip and lower limbs while balancing on 1 foot.

**Variation**

This exercise can also be done by balancing on the ground if you do not have blocks.

**Coaching Points**

1. Demonstrate the correct technique for this exercise.
2. This is designed to loosen up the hip joint and increase flexibility.

---

## Practice 3 — Shooting Practice - '7 Stations'     15-20 mins

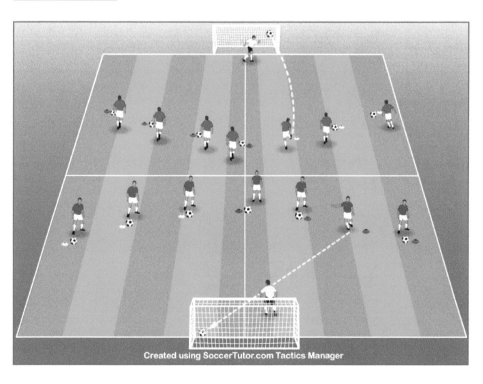

**Description**

Players shoot a stationery ball from different positions. From the red cones the players shoot with their left foot, from the yellow cones they use their right and from the blue cones they shoot with their strongest foot. Set up the exercise with 2 goals to avoid waiting time.

**Variations**

1. Shoot after dribbling.
2. Volley the ball after juggling.
3. Half volley after juggling.

**Coaching Points**

1. Focus the attention on the technique, the body shape and positioning of the non striking foot.
2. Players should use different parts of their feet to shoot depending on the angle.

---

## Practice 4 — Sprinting & Turning in a Shooting Team Game — 20 mins

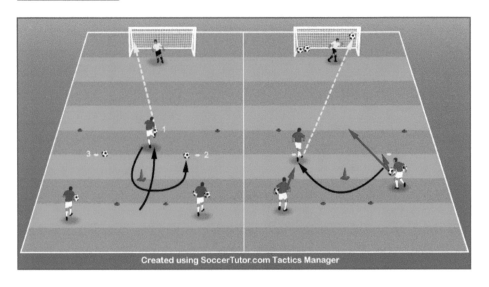

Created using SoccerTutor.com Tactics Manager

### Description

The first player takes 3 consecutive shots. He runs past the cone and shoots he ball closest to the goal.

Then the player runs around the cone as shown and shoots the ball on the right, then does the same for the ball on the left.

While the first player is shooting, the second player in line sets 3 more balls out for their turn.

Each team has only 9 balls so each player must collect the balls quickly. The teams compete against each other.

### Variation

Shoot the ball placed on top of the cone.

### Coaching Points

1. Players should use both feet to shoot in this practice.
2. The head should be over the ball and the back straight when striking.

---

## Practice 5 — 7v7 'Shooting Bonus' Zonal Small Sided Game — 25 mins

After a goal is scored the team has 3 bonus shots available from behind the shooting line. Players taking shots must rotate

Created using SoccerTutor.com Tactics Manager

### Description

We play a 7v7 game where the players can only shoot when they have dribbled into the end zone and then passed the ball to a teammate to finish.

After a goal is scored, the team is allowed 3 bonus shots with stationary balls behind the shooting line.

Players taking the shots must rotate.

### Variation

Allow the teams to shoot after they have completed 7 consecutive passes.

---

## Practice 6 — Free Small Sided Game — 20 mins

**Primary Technical objective:** Shooting.

**Coordination Objective:** Balancing on one foot.

**Secondary Technical Objective:** Receiving, volleying and crossing.

**Tactical Objective:** Creating space.

**Duration of Session:** 85-100 minutes

We recommend starting the session with exercises for general mobility to prevent injuries.

## Practice 1   Juggling on the Move and Finishing   10 mins

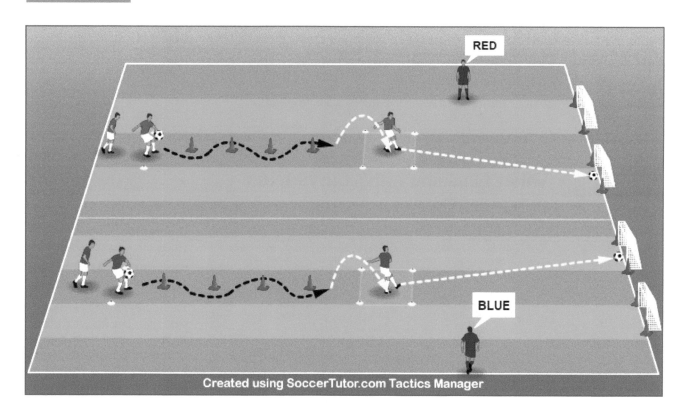

### Description

The player juggles the ball around the cones and then chips the ball up into the receiving area (square).

After controlling the ball, the player shoots making sure to keep the ball low (on the ground).

The shot will either be in the blue or red goal which is called out by the coach.

### Variations

1. Juggling with the thigh.
2. Juggling with only the right foot or left foot.

### Coaching Points

1. The accuracy of the shot and not the power is the focus in this practice.
2. The chip up before the volley should be high and in front of the player to move onto and strike.

## Practice 2   Coordination and Balance with Finishing    10 mins

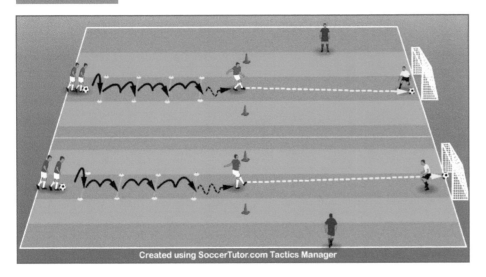

Created using SoccerTutor.com Tactics Manager

### Description

With this coordination exercise we want the player to focus on the planting of their foot (springing and changing direction off one foot).

The player runs with the ball and they must over emphasise the planting of one foot every time it is in line with the cones. The exercise ends with a shot on goal.

It is recommended to make this game a competition between teams of 3 or 4.

### Variation

Shoot with the weaker foot.

### Coaching Points

1. We want quick and sharp changes of direction.

2. The players should take smaller steps when moving forward to shoot.

---

## Practice 3   Volley Finishing with a Curved Run    15-20 mins

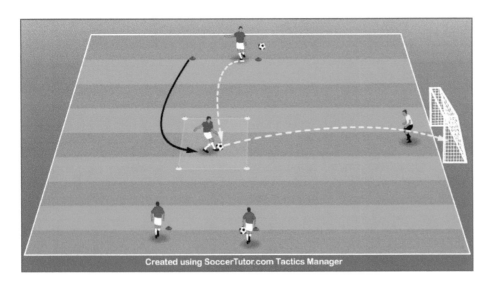

Created using SoccerTutor.com Tactics Manager

### Description

The first player makes a curved run through the back of the centre square.

The second player on that side chips the ball into the square for the first player to volley the ball with the instep at goal.

The player then takes the ball and gets into line on the opposite site.

The players on the opposite side then repeat the same sequence.

### Variation

Receive the ball with the chest and volley or half-volley.

### Coaching Points

1. The players need to watch the ball closely out of the air and onto their foot.

2. Use all parts of the feet, thighs, chest and head to maximise control of the ball.

## Practice 4    Crossing and Finishing with Defensive Pressure    20 mins

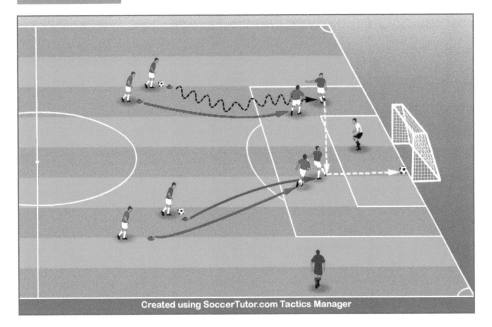

Created using SoccerTutor.com Tactics Manager

### Description

The blue players attack and the red players defend starting from a position of disadvantage. The cross and the shot on goal is made with pressure from behind.

### Variation

The cross is made from a stationery position and both players (blue and red) run to the ball. Cross on the ground.

### Coaching Points

1. Good dribbling and close control is needed at the sides to win the 1v1.

2. The attackers need to show good timing with their runs into the box so they can finish first time.

## Practice 5    Quick Shooting in a 3v3 Small Sided Game    20 mins

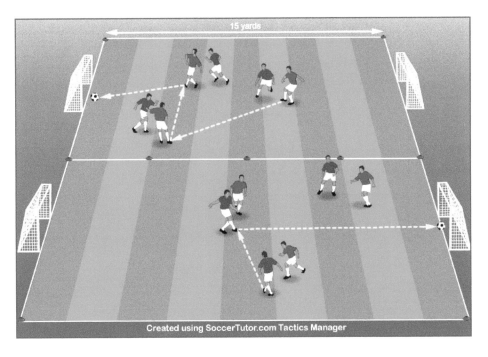

15 yards

Created using SoccerTutor.com Tactics Manager

### Description

A 3v3 game is played in a small area 15 yards long with the objective to score as many goals as possible.

The only rule is that at least 1 pass is required before shooting.

### Variations

1. Goals must be scored from a first time shot.

2. A goal is only allowed after a 1-2 combination.

## Practice 6    Free Small Sided Game    20 mins

**Primary Technical objective:** Shooting.

**Coordination Objective:** Balance and quickness.

**Secondary Technical Objective:** Acrobatic shooting, accuracy, passing and crossing

**Tactical Objective:** Creating space.

**Duration of Session:** 85-100 minutes

We recommend starting the session with exercises for general mobility to prevent injuries.

| Practice 1 | Acrobatic Shooting Game | 10 mins |

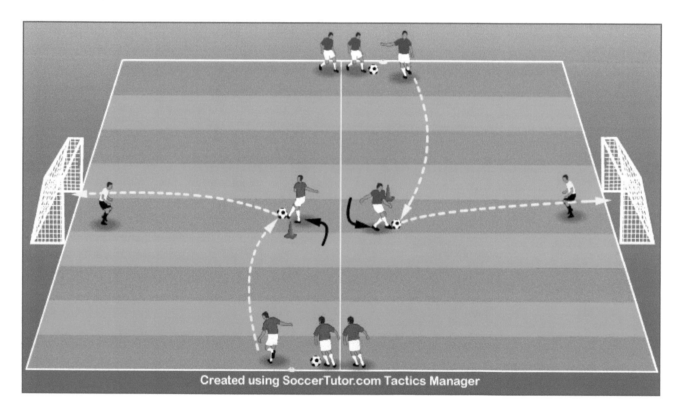

Created using SoccerTutor.com Tactics Manager

### Description

Divide the team into 2 groups. 1 player without the ball stands close to the cone and the other players stand on the side with a ball each.

The exercise starts with a pass to the player on the cone and he shoots with his right foot using a half bicycle kick. He then retrieves the ball and goes to the end of the line. The team with the most goals win the game.

### Variations

**1)** Half bicycle kick with the left foot. **2)** Bicycle kick. **3)** Receive the ball with the chest and volley the ball.

### Coaching Points

1. The accuracy and height of the pass is key to enable the player to take an acrobatic shot.

2. The players need to watch the ball extremely closely to make a good connection with a bicycle kick.

## Practice 2  Coordination & Speed Shooting Practice

**10 mins**

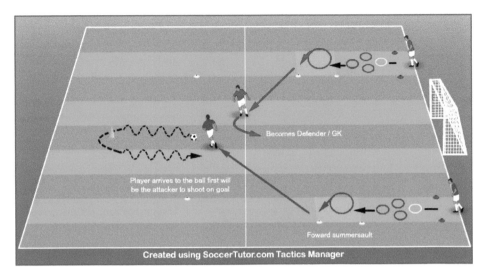

### Description

The players skip over the rings using 1 or 2 feet, do a forward roll and then sprint towards the ball.

Whoever arrives first to the ball dribbles round the cone as shown and then shoots on goal. The other player becomes the goalkeeper.

### Variation

Perform a cartwheel instead of a forward roll.

---

## Practice 3  One Touch Shooting Practice

**15-20 mins**

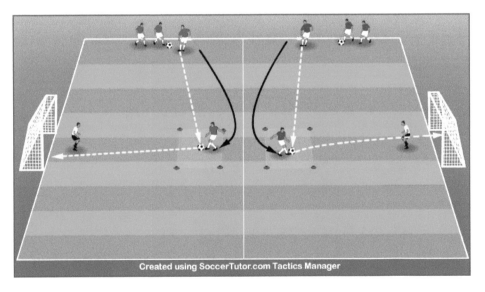

### Description

The first player in line runs round the nearest cone, moves into the square and shoots at goal first time.

They then collect the ball and run back to the end of the line.

The shot is taken with the inside of the foot and the pass from the teammate must be a pass on the ground with pace.

Repeat the exercise from the opposite site.

### Variations

1. Chip pass and header.
2. Chip pass with a half-bicycle kick on the run.
3. Chip pass with a full bicycle kick on the run.
4. Chip pass with chest control and volley.

## Practice 4   2v1 on the Flank and 1v1 in the Box     20 mins

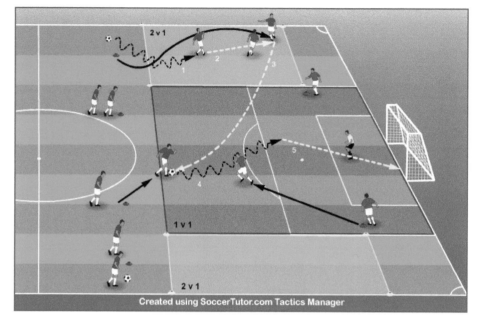

### Description

The blue players are positioned in 4 stations and the reds in 2 (as in the diagram).

The blue players have a 2v1 advantage on the flank with the aim to cross the ball to their teammate in the middle using an overlap.

The red defender is passive.

The red player defends actively in the 1v1 area when the blue player tries to shoot on goal.

### Variation

Active defending in the 2v1 area.

### Coaching Points

1.  Players should try to get their shot off early in the 1v1 situation.
2.  Use a feint/move to beat so they can work the space for a shot.

## Practice 5   1v1 Marking in a 4v4 Small Sided Game     20 mins

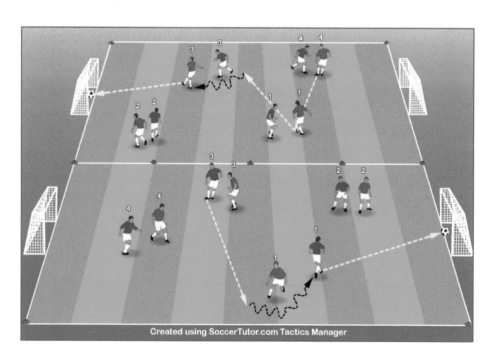

### Description

He we have a 4v4 tournament. Each player is assigned 1 player to mark.

If a player beats their defender then they can shoot freely as no other player can mark or tackle them.

### Variation

Mark out a shooting area on the pitch.

## Practice 6   Free Small Sided Game     20 mins

**Primary Technical objective:** Shooting.

**Coordination Objective:** Balance, quickness, space/time adaptation and transformation.

**Secondary Technical Objective:** Receiving the ball and shooting with accuracy.

**Tactical Objective:** Creating space.

**Duration of Session:** 85-100 minutes

We recommend starting the session with exercises for general mobility to prevent injuries.

---

**Practice 1**   **Shooting Accuracy with Throw-ins**   **10 mins**

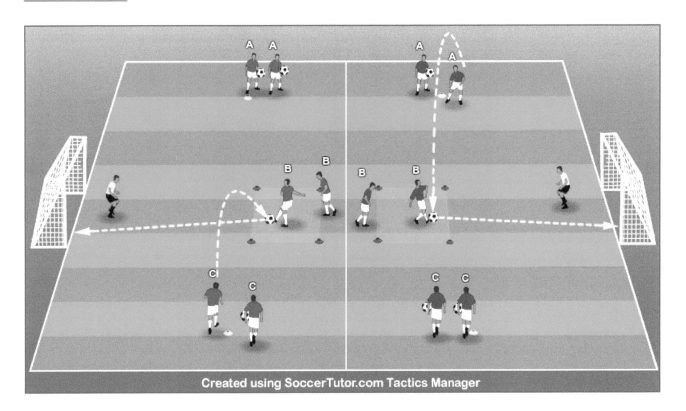

Created using SoccerTutor.com Tactics Manager

### Description

Each team have 6 players as shown in the diagram. Player A uses the throw-in technique to throw the ball to player B within the square who shoots at goal with the inside of the foot.

Players use all parts of both feet during this practice (determined by the coach).

### Variation

Receive the ball with the chest and shoot.

### Coaching Points

1. Players must focus on accuracy and not power in this practice.

2. They must shoot standing on the spot within the square.

3. As the players shooting are stationary, so the accuracy and flight of the throw are very important.

---

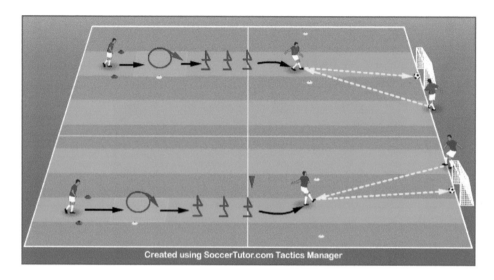

### Description

Players start by doing a forward roll, then jump over the hurdles, run towards the ball and shoot with 1 touch.

This is a team game and the team with the most goals wins the competition.

### Variation

Chip pass and shoot with a volley.

### Coaching Points

1. Good rhythm and balance is needed in the transition from the roll to jumping over the hurdles.
2. Players should use small steps up to the cones before shooting first time, for a more controlled shot.

---

**Practice 3**    **Pass, Receive and Shoot on the Turn**    **15-20 mins**

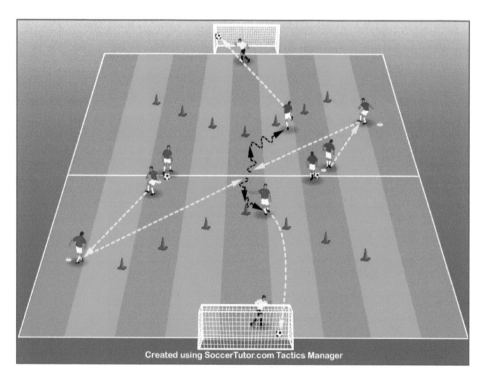

### Description

The first player passes the ball to their teammate, who passes the ball to the other player waiting in the middle.

That player runs round the first cone, sends the ball slightly ahead of it, turns and shoots at goal. The next player shoots from the next cone over.

Players shoot from all the cones using their right and left foot.

Players move to the next position.

### Variation

Running with the ball without sending the ball ahead of the cone, assign a number to the cone and indicate the player which cone he needs to shoot from.

---

## Practice 4 — Sprint, Change Direction and Shooting Race — 20 mins

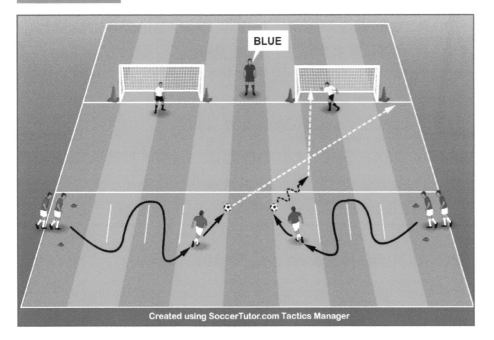

**Description**

Players are divided into 2 groups and 2 players start the drill at the same time.

The first players in line run round the poles as shown which are laid on the ground and then sprint to the ball.

The coach then calls out the colour of the goal to shoot into and the first player to score gets 1 point for their team.

**Variations**

1. Use rings instead of poles.
2. Indicate the goal to shoot in with visual signs.

## Practice 5 — Shooting Practice in a 7v7 Possession Game — 20 mins

**Description**

2 teams of 7 play with the aim to keep possession inside the central zone.

The first aim is to keep possession and complete 5 passes.

At this point, the last player to receive the ball can shoot without any pressure from the opponents.

The shot must be taken within the central zone.

**Variations**

1. Change the number of minimum passes.
2. Play possession with a combination of hands and feet.

## Practice 6 — Free Small Sided Game — 20 mins

**Primary Technical objective:** Shooting.

**Coordination Objective:** Balance, quickness, differentiation, adaptation and transformation.

**Secondary Technical Objective:** Running with the ball.

**Tactical Objective:** Creating space.

**Duration of Session:** 85-100 minutes

We recommend starting the session with exercises for general mobility to prevent injuries.

| Practice 1 | Dribble, Shoot, Turn, Receive and Shoot Again | 10 mins |

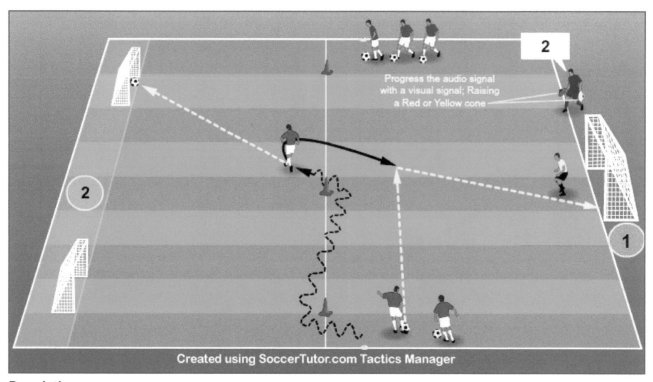

Created using SoccerTutor.com Tactics Manager

### Description

The player runs with the ball round the cones as shown and the coach calls number 1 (indicating the big goal) or number 2 (indicating the small goals) which the player must shoot into. The players need accuracy to score in the smaller goals and need to beat the goalkeeper in the big goal.

The player then moves to receive a pass from their teammate to shoot on the opposite side (at the big goal in the diagram, after having shot in the small goal). Run the drill from both sides.

### Variation

Substitute the audio signal with a visual signal (coloured cones shown in the diagram).

### Coaching Points

1. This practice should be done at a high tempo.

2. During the dribbling part, the player should first run quickly with the ball before slowing down, using small touches to turn around the cone and then shoot.

3. The pass should be well weighted, so the ball is played in front of the player to turn and run onto.

## Practice 2 — Speed & Agility Shooting Competition — 10 mins

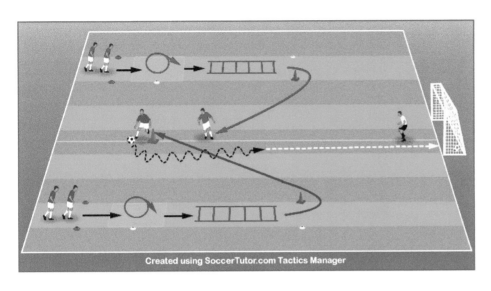

Created using SoccerTutor.com Tactics Manager

### Description

The first player from each group performs a forward roll, runs through the ladder using diagonal steps (left foot step on the right and right foot step on the left).

Both players run around the cone and race to the ball.

The first player to the ball aims to score in the goal.

The other player becomes the defender (1v1 +GK).

### Variations

1. Introduce a second ball.
2. Use speed rings instead of ladders.
3. Substitute the forward roll with a side roll.

## Practice 3 — Shooting Accuracy - 'Aim for a Corner' — 15-20 mins

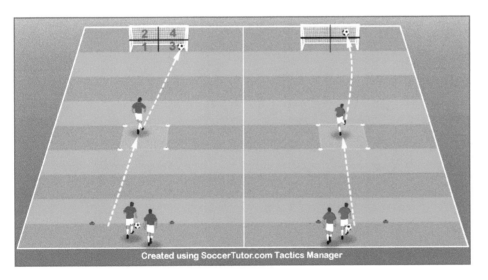

Created using SoccerTutor.com Tactics Manager

### Description

The first player of each group passes the ball into the square and follows their own pass to shoot at goal. The shot must be inside the square.

Tape is used on the goals to divide it into 4 corners. The player calls out 1,2,3 or 4 before shooting and aims for that corner, winning a point if successful.

### Variations

1) The area of the goal to shoot in is called out by the coach. 2) The pass to themselves can be in the air.

### Coaching Points

1. The accuracy and weight of the pass is important so that the ball is within the square for the shot.
2. Players should sprint forwards and then slow down to take smaller steps before striking the ball.

## Practice 4   Running Backwards, Dribbling & Shooting Game   20 mins

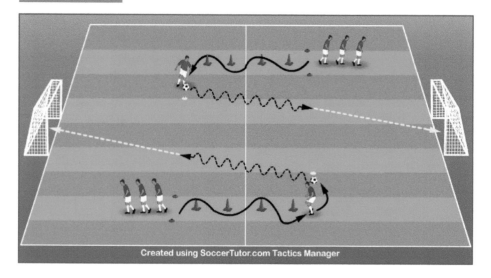

Created using SoccerTutor.com Tactics Manager

### Description

Players run backwards through the cones, turn and sprint to the ball.

They then run with the ball towards the opposite goal and shoot.

Players start at the same time and the first player to score a goal gets 3 points, the second 1 point if they score.

### Variations

1. Substitute the shot for a 1v1 with the a goalkeeper.
2. Run forwards through the cones or laterally.

### Coaching Point

1. When running backwards players should use small steps to maintain their balance and coordination.

---

## Practice 5   Shooting Accuracy in a 6v6 Small Side Game   20 mins

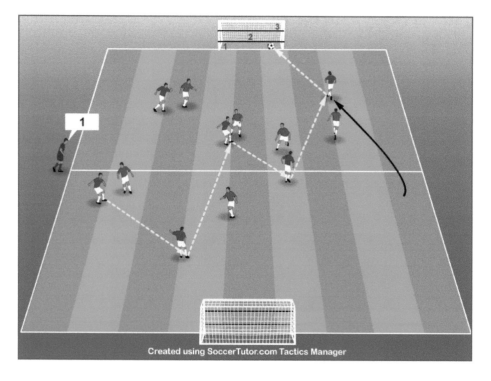

Created using SoccerTutor.com Tactics Manager

### Description

Players play a regular 6v6 small sided game but without goalkeepers.

The goal is marked with tape and separated into 3 zones horizontally.

A goal is only valid if it is scored in the zone called out by the coach.

The coach will constantly change the zone the players are aiming for.

### Variations

1. Assign different points to the different areas.
2. Introduce penalty or a point for the opposing team if the goal is scored in the wrong zone.

## Practice 6   Free Small Sided Game   20 mins

**Primary Technical objective:** Volleys.

**Coordination Objective:** Balancing on one foot, quickness, planting the foot and reading the trajectory of the ball.

**Secondary Technical Objective:** Running with the ball and directional receiving of the ball.

**Tactical Objective:** Defend the goal and feints .

**Duration of Session:** 85-100 minutes

We recommend starting the session with exercises for general mobility to prevent injuries.

---

| Practice 1 | Volleying Accuracy - 'Aim for a Corner' | 10 mins |
|---|---|---|

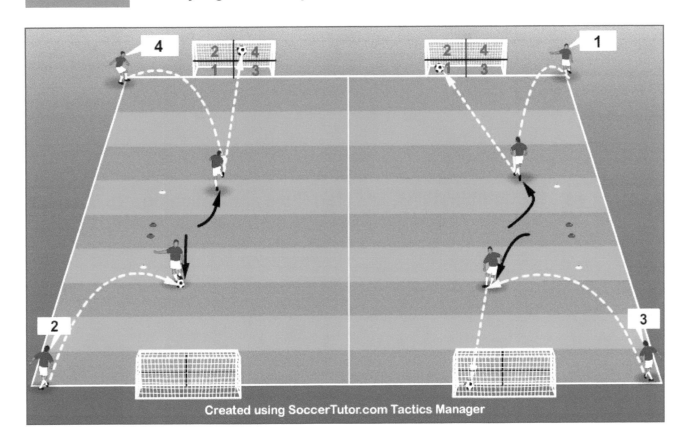

Created using SoccerTutor.com Tactics Manager

### Description

The players are divided into 4 groups. Each group of players stand in front of a goal (small goals can be used). The first player runs toward the ball and volleys the ball chipped by the player on the side.

The goal is divided into 4 zones with tape. The player chipping the ball from the side calls out a number and the player shooting must aim for the zone called out by the teammate.

### Variations

**1)** Heading. **2)** Receiving with the chest and volley. **3)** Volley with inside of foot. **4)** Volley with instep.

### Coaching Points

1. The accuracy and flight of the pass is key for the players to be able to move forward and volley the ball.

2. When volleying, the players heads should be over the ball and their back should be straight.

---

## Practice 2    Speed Ring Coordination Relay     10 mins

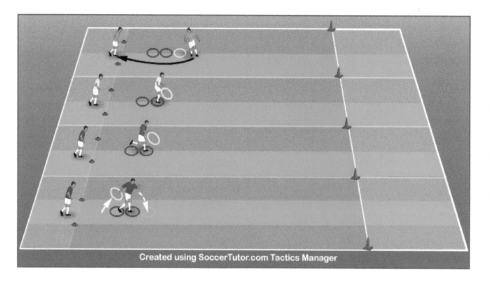

Created using SoccerTutor.com Tactics Manager

### Description

The first player in the line picks up the first ring, skips/hops through the other rings on 1 foot, drops the ring at the end of the line and sprints back to high five their teammate who then goes.

The team that moves the rings to the finish line first wins the competition.

### Coaching Points

1. This relay should be done at a high tempo as it is a competition.

2. This exercise works on the players coordination, moving up, down and changing direction.

## Practice 3    1-2 Combinations, 3rd Man Runs and Finishing    15-20 mins

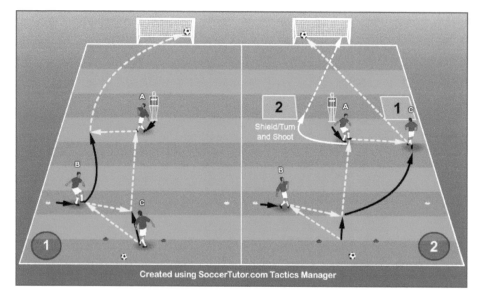

Created using SoccerTutor.com Tactics Manager

### Description

Player C plays a 1-2 combination with Player B and passes to Player A.

Player A has 2 options:

1. Pass to player B who runs forward and shoots.

2. 2. Pass to player C who runs forward and shoots.

Make the exercise a competition between 2 teams.

### Variations

1. Player A receives the ball, shields the ball, then turns and shoots (this is Option 2 in the second part of the diagram on the right half).

2. Use chip passes with a volley at the end.

3. Receiving the ball with the chest and bicycle kick.

## Practice 4 — 1-2 Combination and 1v1 Duel — 20 mins

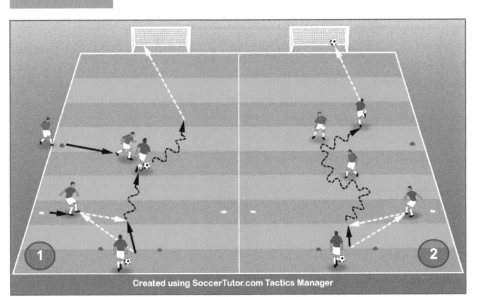

### Description

The blue player plays a 1-2 combination with their teammate and dribbles the ball forwards.

The red player then moves across to apply passive pressure trying to prevent a direct shot at goal.

The attacking player uses a series of feints and changes of direction to work enough space to shoot in the goal.

Change the roles often.

### Variation

Introduce a second defender for a 1v2 duel (as shown in part 2 of the diagram).

## Practice 5 — Possession Game with Quick Attack & Finishing — 15-20 mins

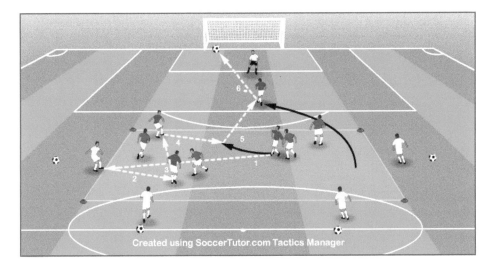

### Description

Divide the group into 3 teams. In an area 20 x 20 yards, 2 teams of 4-6 players play a game while the other team stand outside on 3 sides of the square.

The teams must shoot after their 3rd pass. If a goal is scored before the 3 pass, the goal is considered an own goal.

The players on the outside play with the team in possession and pass new balls into the game when the ball goes out.

### Variation

Goal is only valid after a 1-2 combination or with a first time shot.

### Coaching Points

1. Correct body shape (open up on the half turn) and positioning is important to view where the next pass is going.

2. The timing of the final pass and the run need to be well coordinated.

## Practice 6 — Free Small Sided Game — 20 mins

**Primary Technical objective:** Volleys.

**Coordination Objective:** Balance on one foot, quickness, planting the foot and reading the trajectory of the ball.

**Secondary Technical Objective:** Running with the ball and directional receiving of the ball.

**Tactical Objective:** Defend the goal and feints.

**Duration of Session:** 85-100 minutes

We recommend starting the session with exercises for general mobility to prevent injuries.

---

**Practice 1** Throw, Catch and Volley in a 4v4 Game                 **10 mins**

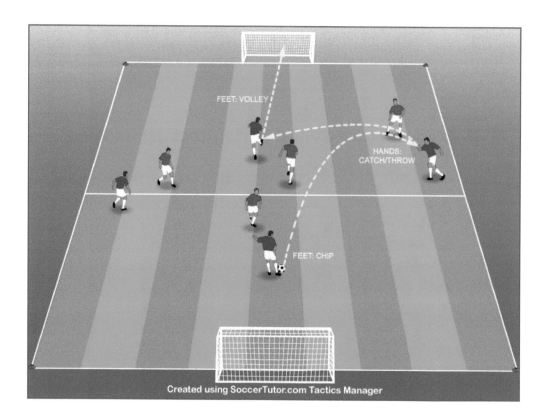

### Description

Play a game where every pass with the hands (throw and catch) is followed by a pass with a volley. A goal is only allowed with a volley.

It is also allowed to make more consecutive passes with the feet but as soon as the ball hits the ground, possession passes to the other team.

If a goal is scored after 2 consecutive volley passes, the goal counts double.

### Variations

1. A goal can only be scored with the feet.
2. A goal can only be scored with the head.
3. A goal can only be scored with an acrobatic shot.

---

## Practice 2    Agility Circuit with 1 Touch Finishing     10 mins

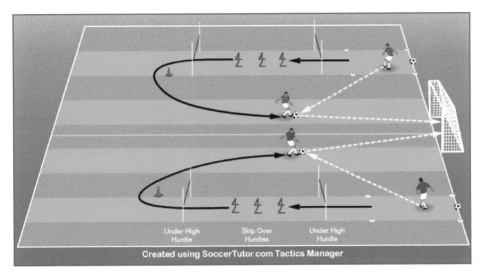

**Description**

The player starts without the ball, crawls under the high obstacle, jumps over the low hurdles, crawls under the next high obstacle and runs towards the goal.

A teammate then passes the ball across and the player shoots first time into the goal.

### Variation

Use a chip pass and directional control, shooting a bouncing ball with a half volley.

### Coaching Points

1. The run and the pass need to be well coordinated so that the speed of play is maximised.

2. Going under then over the obstacles before running and shooting is good for coordination training.

## Practice 3    Passing & Receiving in a Shooting Practice     15-20 mins

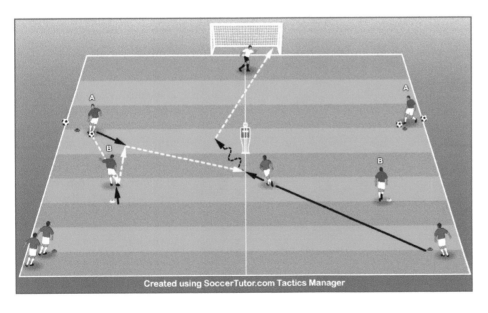

**Description**

Player A plays a 1-2 with Player B, then plays the ball into the centre to the red player who sprints up from the corner.

The red player controls the ball and shoots at goal quickly. The players exchange positions.

Repeat the exercise with the other foot from the opposite side.

### Variations

1. Pass in the air.

2. Receive with the chest and shoot.

3. Pass in the air, trap the ball with the sole of the foot and shoot.

4. Pass in the air, receive in the air with the inside of the foot and shoot.

## Practice 4 — 3v4 (+2) Attackers vs Defenders Shooting Drill    20 mins

Created using SoccerTutor.com Tactics Manager

### Description

3 defenders play against 4 attackers in a zone outside the penalty area with 3 outside neutral players for support.

The attackers must use their numerical advantage to make movements, creating space to shoot at goal.

### Variation

Introduce another defender.

### Coaching Points

1. The correct angles and distance of supporting players from the man in possession are key to provide options.
2. The timing of the pass and the run need to be coordinated (communication), as well as quality finishing.

---

## Practice 5 — 7v7 (+6) with Outside Support in a SSG    20 mins

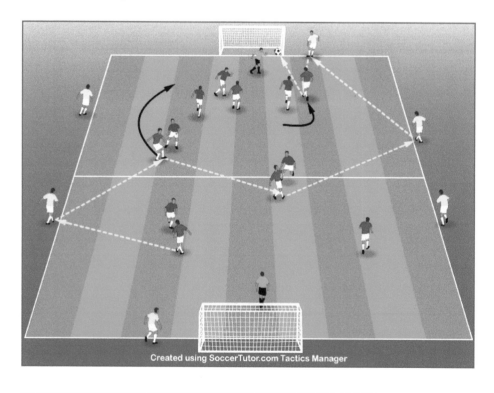

Created using SoccerTutor.com Tactics Manager

### Description

Divide the group into 3 teams of 7.

2 teams play a 7v7 game.

The yellow team (neutral) are positioned on the outside of the pitch as shown in the diagram.

A goal is only valid after a pass or cross from an outside player (yellow) and must be a first time shot.

### Variation

Play a hand ball game with a goal only valid with a volley after a pass from an outside player.

---

## Practice 6    Free Small Sided Game    20 mins

**Primary Technical objective:** Shooting.

**Coordination Objective:** Differentiation and quickness.

**Secondary Technical Objective:** Passing in the air and throw-ins.

**Tactical Objective:** Dribbling and defending the goal.

**Duration of Session:** 85-100 minutes

We recommend starting the session with exercises for general mobility to prevent injuries.

---

| Practice 1 | Pass, Throw, Chip and Accurate Volley | 10 mins |

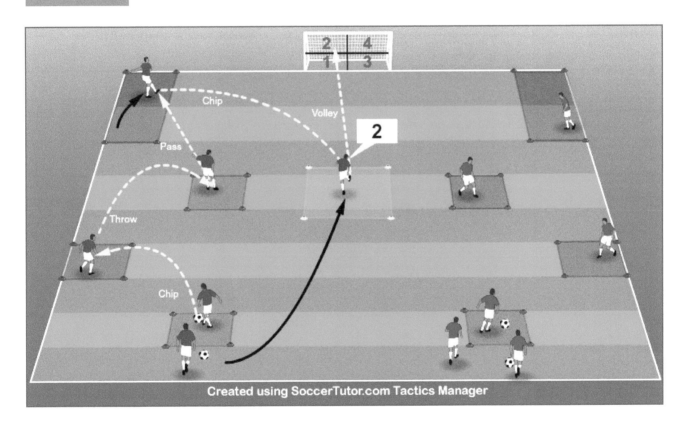

Created using SoccerTutor.com Tactics Manager

## Description

Players in a team make a sequence of consecutive passes. The first is a chip, then a throw, then a pass and finally a chip for a volley on goal. The passes must be into the square areas.

The player shooting will call the number assigned to the section of the goal where they intend to shoot.

## Variations

1. Finish with a header.
2. Finish with a half-volley.
3. Receive with the chest and shoot on the volley.

## Coaching Points

1. The final chip pass and the run into the final square has to be very well timed and coordinated.
2. This practice can be done with just chip passes if the age/level is appropriate.

---

## Practice 2 — Roll, Dribble and Shoot with a Goalkeeper

**10 mins**

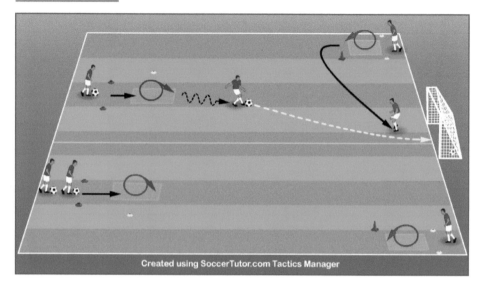

Created using SoccerTutor.com Tactics Manager

### Description

The blue player performs a forward roll, dribbles forward and shoots at goal.

The red player performs a roll, then runs round the cone to become the goalkeeper and stop the blue player from scoring.

### Variation

Substitute the forward roll with a side roll.

### Coaching Points

1. When performing the forward roll, the players can trap the ball in between their feet.

2. The shot should be taken as early as possible in this practice before the goalkeeper can settle.

---

## Practice 3 — Penalty Kick Practice

**15-20 mins**

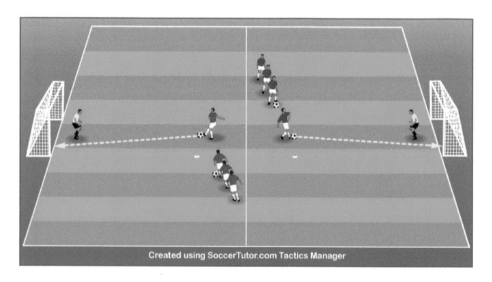

Created using SoccerTutor.com Tactics Manager

### Description

Players practice taking penalty kicks against a goalkeeper.

### Variations

1. Use the weaker foot.

2. Powerful shot.

3. Accurate shot.

### Coaching Points

1. The non-striking foot should be placed next to the ball when shooting.

2. The head should be over the ball and the back straight.

---

## Practice 4 | 1v2 Dynamic Duel with 3 Goals | 20 mins

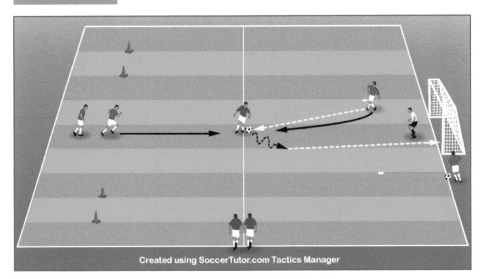

Created using SoccerTutor.com Tactics Manager

### Description

In an area 25 yards long, the blue player stands in the middle. The defenders stand at a distance of 8 yards from the attacker.

One of the defenders passes the ball to the attacker and then closes him down. The other defender closes him down from the opposite end.

The attacker aims to beat the defender/s and score past the goalkeeper. The defenders can score by winning the ball, then dribbling and shooting in either of the 2 small goals on the opposite side.

### Variations

1. 2 defenders start from 1 side of the area both applying pressure from behind.

2. Increase the distance of the defenders and use an aerial pass into the middle.

### Coaching Point

1. The player should take a directional first touch when receiving and then try to quickly work the space to shoot before pressure is applied by 2 defenders.

---

## Practice 5 | 7v7 Shooting Area 6 Goals Small Sided Game | 15-20 mins

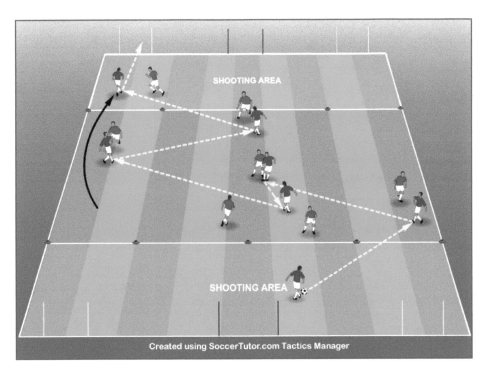

SHOOTING AREA

SHOOTING AREA

Created using SoccerTutor.com Tactics Manager

### Description

We have a 7v7 game with the players using a maximum of 2 touches.

Both teams can score in any of the 3 goals they are attacking.

All shots must be made from within the shooting area.

If a player scores from outside the shooting area, it counts as an own goal.

### Variations

1. A goal is only valid if the shot is hit along the ground.

2. A goal is only valid from an aerial shot.

---

## Practice 6 | Free Small Sided Game | 20 mins

---

**Primary Technical objective:** Volleying with accuracy.

**Coordination Objective:** Reading the trajectory of the ball, adaptation, quickness and orientation.

**Secondary Technical Objective:** Running with the ball, penetrating passes, passing in the air and receiving.

**Tactical Objective:** Feints and creating space.

**Duration of Session:** 85-100 minutes

---

We recommend starting the session with exercises for general mobility to prevent injuries.

---

| Practice 1 | Throw, Catch and Volley in a 4v4 Game | 10 mins |

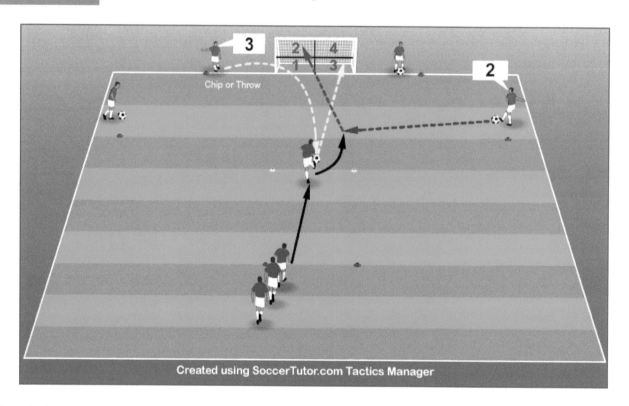

Created using SoccerTutor.com Tactics Manager

### Description

Players run up to the line as shown and volley the ball from a throw-in by their teammate who is standing at the side of the goal. The thrower calls out a number corresponding to the section of the goal where the player shooting must direct the ball.

A second ball is then passed in from the side and the player must quickly react to shoot first time again. The player who passed again calls out a number corresponding to the section of the goal where the player shooting must direct the ball.

The goals are only valid if the ball is scored in the section called out.

### Variations

1. Headers instead of a volley.

2. Half volley.

3. Chip the ball for the pass instead of a throw-in (as shown in diagram).

---

## Practice 2 — Turn and Shoot First Time

**10 mins**

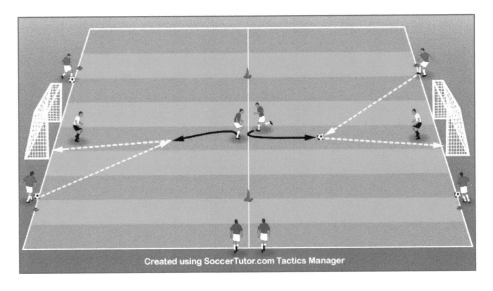

Created using SoccerTutor.com Tactics Manager

**Description**

The blue players stand with their back to goal.

The red players stand either side of the goals with a ball to pass into the middle.

As the blue players hear the ball being passed by the red player, they turn and shoot first time.

### Variation

Pass the ball with a chip and only allow 1 bounce before striking the ball

### Coaching Points

1. Quick reactions are needed to turn and then shoot instantly.
2. The pass should be accurate and well weighted for the player to be able to strike first time.

---

## Practice 3 — Feints / Quick Movements and Shot

**15-20 mins**

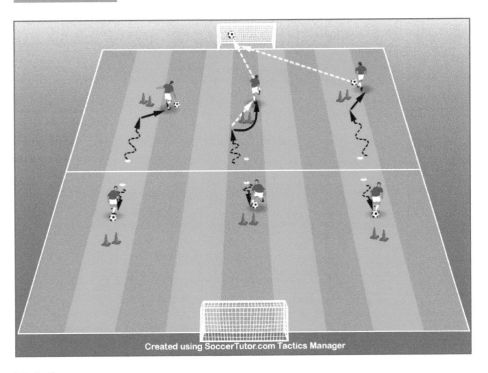

Created using SoccerTutor.com Tactics Manager

**Description**

In this practice player practice feints followed by a shot from the positions of the cones.

On the outside cones (left/right), make a feint and go towards the outside of the cones and shoot.

On the central cones, the player passes the ball to the left of the cones, runs round the right of them to meet the ball and shoot.

### Variations

1. Feint and then cut inside on the outside cones.
2. Feint from a stationery position and shoot immediately.

---

## Practice 4    3v2 First Time Shooting Practice     20 mins

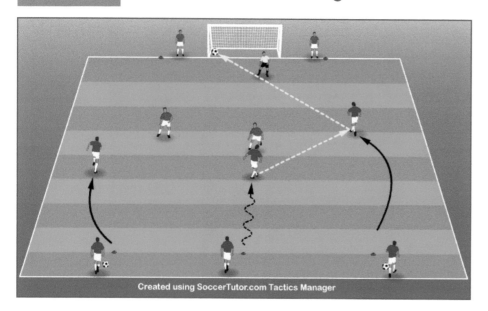

Created using SoccerTutor.com Tactics Manager

### Description

3 attackers start the game with the ball against 3 defenders.

Once the 2nd defender decides to close down one of the players without the ball, the player in possession must pass to the player free in space, who must receive and shoot on goal.

### Variation

Modify the starting position of the 3 attackers, 1 with their back to goal and 2 facing the goal.

## Practice 5    2 Team Accurate Passing and Finishing Game    20 mins

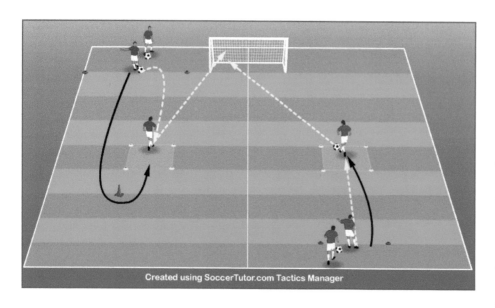

Created using SoccerTutor.com Tactics Manager

### Description

The blue players must run round the cone as shown and then volley the ball after a chip pass from their teammate. The goal is only valid if the ball is passed within the square.

The red players pass the ball to themselves from the opposite end into the square, run forwards and shoot. The shot must again be hit within the square.

The team that scores the most goals in a set amount of time wins the game.

### Variations

1. Pass into the square on the ground.
2. Move the square closer and score with headers after a throw-in.
3. Acrobatic shooting after throw-ins.

### Coaching Point

1. Players should sprint up to the cone, then slow down and bend the knees to turn around it (change direction).

## Practice 6    Free Small Sided Game     20 mins

# CHAPTER

## 6

# Heading Training Unit

**Primary Technical objective:** Heading.

**Coordination Objective:** Quickness, motor skills (jumping), dynamic balance and trajectory.

**Secondary Technical Objective:** Throw-ins and crossing.

**Tactical Objective:** Marking, creating space and 1v1s.

**Duration of Session:** 85-100 minutes

We recommend starting the session with exercises for general mobility to prevent injuries.

---

**Practice 1** | **Heading Accuracy – 'Aim for the Ring'** | **10 mins**

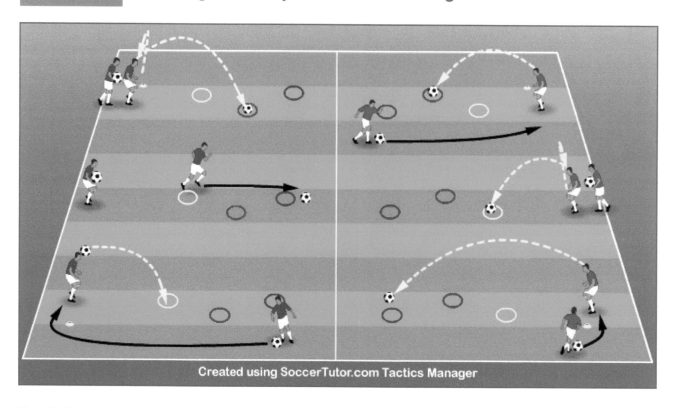

Created using SoccerTutor.com Tactics Manager

### Description

Each player throws the ball in the air and heads it towards one of the rings positioned at various distances (3 yards, 5 yards, 7 yards).

Assign a point to the rings based on the distance and colour.

The team with the most points win the game.

### Variation

The ball is kicked up in the air and then headed (instead of thrown).

### Coaching Points

1. Players should get good height on their throws/kicks so that they are able to jump up and head the ball.
2. These headers should be made with the middle of the forehead.

---

## Practice 2 · Agility and Heading Competition

**10 mins**

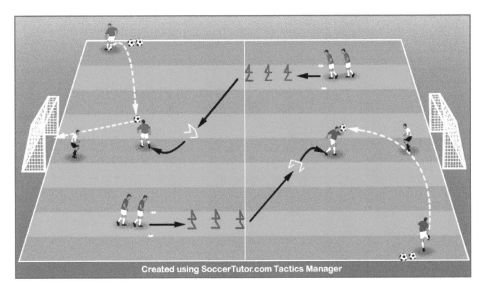

**Description**

Each player jumps over the first 3 red hurdles, then runs to jump over the yellow hurdle.

After completing the obstacle part, the player heads the ball which is passed by a teammate on the side with a throw-in.

Progress to crossing with feet rather than throw-ins (as shown in the diagram).

**Variation**

Diving header.

**Coaching Points**

1. The cross needs to be accurate and enable the players to jump and head the ball.
2. The hurdles are good practice for jumping off the ground and maintaining balance for heading.

## Practice 3 · Diving Headers in Pairs

**15-20 mins**

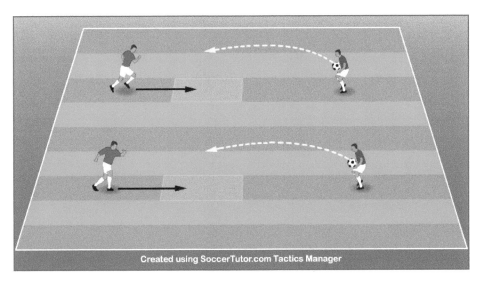

**Description**

Players move forward and perform a diving header from a ball thrown by their teammate.

Change roles often.

**Variation**

Head from a kneeling position (on their knees).

**Coaching Points**

1. The accuracy and height of the throw is key for the players to be able to perform a diving header.
2. Make sure players use their hands to break their fall to avoid any injuries.

## Practice 4  1v1 Heading in the Penalty Area

**20 mins**

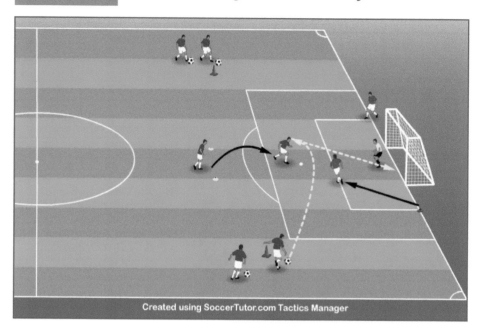

Created using SoccerTutor.com Tactics Manager

### Description

The blue players cross the ball from the side of the penalty area.

There is a 1v1 situation in the penalty area with 1 attacker vs 1 defender. The aim is to score with a header.

A headed goal counts double.

### Variation

The defender is passive.

### Coaching Points

1. The cross and the run need to be well coordinated.
2. When under pressure from a defender, the attacker needs to check away/change direction to create space.

## Practice 5  6v6 Headers Game with 6 Outside Players

**20 mins**

Created using SoccerTutor.com Tactics Manager

### Description

In an area 25 x 20 yards we play a 6v6 handball game with 6 outside support players.

A goal is only valid if it is scored from a header with an assist by an outside player.

Progress to the outside players using their heads (as shown in diagram).

### Variation

Play with hands and feet, kicking the ball out of the hands and catching to pass and receive.

## Practice 6  Free Small Sided Game

**20 mins**

**Primary Technical objective:** Heading.

**Coordination Objective:** Quickness, motor skills (jumping), dynamic balance and trajectory.

**Secondary Technical Objective:** Crossing.

**Tactical Objective:** Marking, creating space, 2v1s and set plays.

**Duration of Session:** 85-100 minutes

We recommend starting the session with exercises for general mobility to prevent injuries.

---

| Practice 1 | 4v4 Headed Finishing Game | 10 mins |

Created using SoccerTutor.com Tactics Manager

### Description

8 players are at the side with a ball and cross one at a time. A goal can be scored by both teams in either of the 2 goals each defended by a goalkeeper.

A goal can only be scored with a header.

### Variation

Goals can be scored with a volley or with an acrobatic shot.

---

## Practice 2 — Jump, Run, Change Direction and Headed Pass — 10 mins

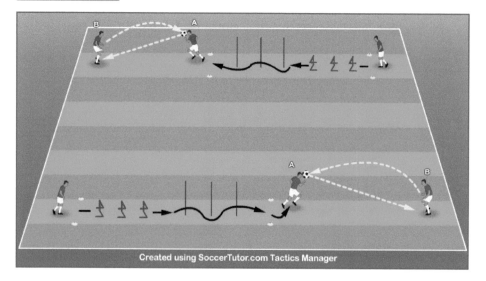

### Description

Player A jumps over the hurdles, runs through the poles as shown and then runs to head the ball thrown by their teammate.

Player A then takes up Player B's position and Player B runs to the starting position at the opposite end.

Make the game a competition.

### Variation

Change the agility circuit.

### Coaching Points

1. Players should take small, quick side-to-side steps through the poles.

2. To head down, the player must jump higher than the ball and lean the head forwards.

---

## Practice 3 — Heading Accuracy 'Aim for a Corner' — 15-20 mins

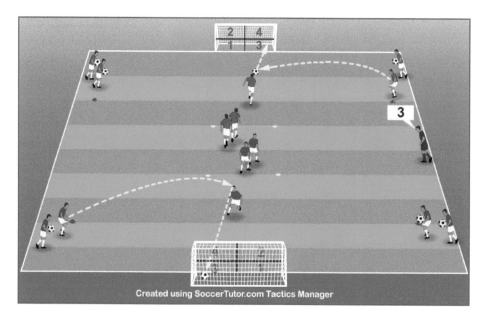

### Description

Divide the goals into various sections with tape and assign a point system to each zone.

The players at the side use a throw-in to pass the ball and the central players must direct their header towards the section of the goal (1,2,3 or 4) called out by the coach.

### Variation

Competitive game with 2 goals (as shown in the diagram).

### Coaching Point

1. The players will have to use different heading techniques and different parts of the head depending on the throw and which section the coach calls out - Middle, side of the head, heading down, diving header etc.

## Practice 4   2v1 with Headed Knock Down and Finishing   20 mins

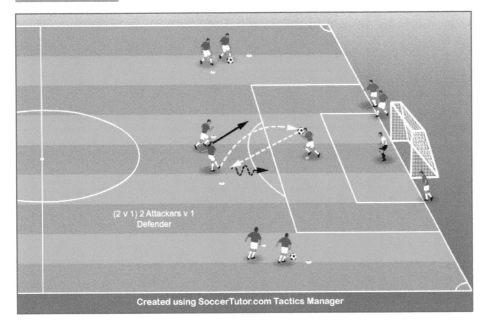

Created using SoccerTutor.com Tactics Manager

### Description

A blue player stands 7-8 yards outside the penalty area and chips the ball to their teammate inside the box.

The red player heads the ball back and the 2 blue players have a 2v1 situation against the red defender.

### Variations

1. Make the defender passive.
2. Add another defender (2v2).

## Practice 5   Heading with Target Players in a Small Sided Game   20 mins

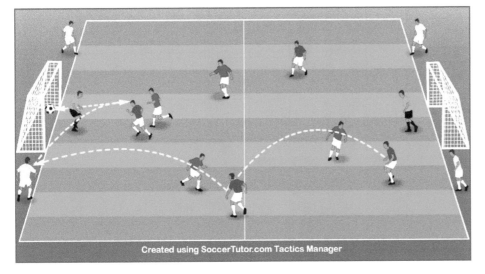

Created using SoccerTutor.com Tactics Manager

### Description

In an area 20 x 25 yards we have a 4v4 (+2 GKs) game.

There are 4 target players who stand either side of the goal (2 at each end).

The objective is to score with a header with an assist from a target player.

The game is played with the hands and head.

Change target players.

### Variations

1. Hands and feet game.
2. Game with only feet.

## Practice 6   Free Small Sided Game   20 mins

**Primary Technical objective:** Heading.

**Coordination Objective:** Power and jumping.

**Secondary Technical Objective:** Crossing.

**Tactical Objective:** Set plays, 2v1s, marking and creating space.

**Duration of Session:** 85-100 minutes

We recommend starting the session with exercises for general mobility to prevent injuries.

---

**Practice 1**    **Heading Accuracy 'Against the Crossbar'**     **10 mins**

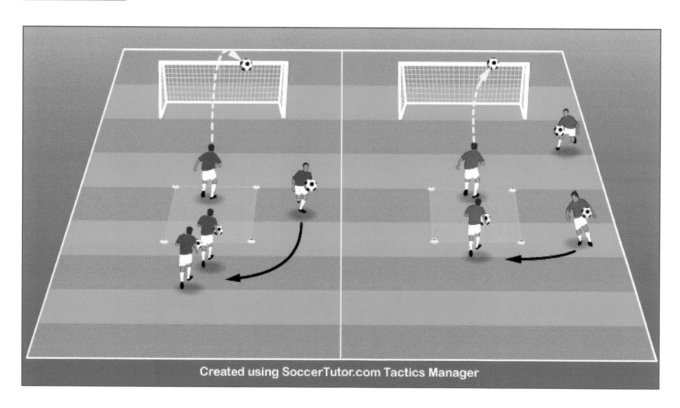

Created using SoccerTutor.com Tactics Manager

### Description

2 teams of 4-5 players compete in a game where the players throw the ball in the air and head the ball trying to hit the crossbar.

### Variation

Substitute a header for a goal with a volley or with an acrobatic shot.

### Coaching Points

1. To head the ball up onto the crossbar, the players need to get under the flight of the ball and use the middle of the forehead.

2. For older or more developed players have them juggle the ball and then kick it up in the air for the header against the crossbar.

---

## Practice 2    Coordination, Agility and Balance Exercise    10 mins

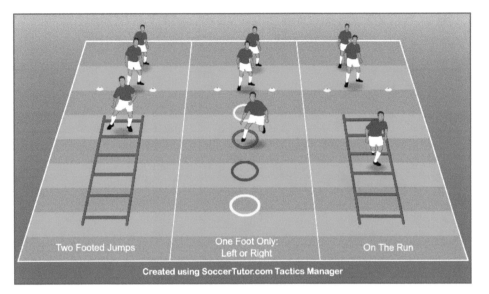

### Description

In this exercise players perform various types of jumping, hopping and running in the speed rings and ladders.

They perform 2 footed jumps with the first ladder, hop on 1 foot through the speed rings and run through the last ladder.

### Variation

Make it a relay competition.

---

## Practice 3    Headed Passing and Shooting Practice    15-20 mins

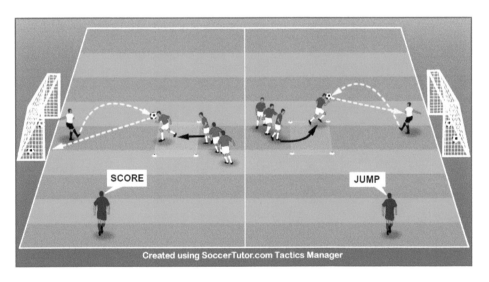

### Description

The goalkeeper chips the ball up into the square which is 7-8 yards in front of the goal.

The players run towards the ball and head it based on what the coach calls:

1. With a jump, the ball must be passed back to the goalkeeper's hands.

2. Without a jump (score), they head at goal towards a corner of the goal.

### Variations

1. Competition with 2 goals.
2. Goalkeeper chips the ball from a side on position.

### Coaching Points

1. Players need good awareness and quick reactions to respond to coach's call.
2. Monitor technique for heading while jumping and while on the ground.

## Practice 4  Throw-ins, Heading, 1v1s and Finishing     **20 mins**

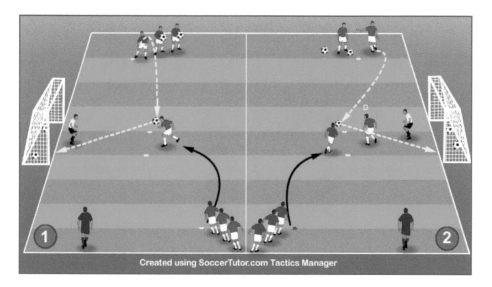

### Variations

1. Diving header.
2. Add a defender to group 1.
3. Cross with feet in group 1.

### Description

*GROUP 1*
The red player starts from the side and runs to the middle and heads at goal from 7-8 yards away from the goal. The ball is thrown by the blue player using a throw-in.

*GROUP 2*
The blue player does the same as the red player in group 1, but faces a defender when trying to head at goal. The red player at the side crosses the ball instead of throwing.

The blues and reds compete and the team that score the most goals win.

---

## Practice 5  Heading with Target Players in a SSG (2)     **20 mins**

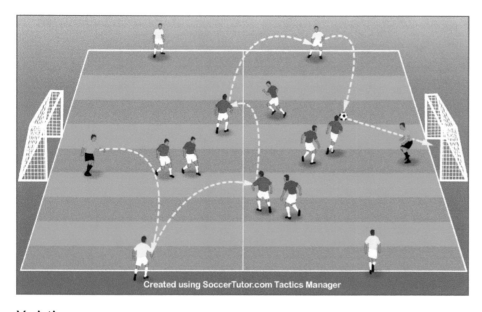

### Variations

1. Hands and feet game.
2. Game with just feet.
3. Headed goal after a headed assist counts as 5 points.

### Description

In an area 20 x 25 yards we have a 4v4 (+2 GKs) game.

There are 4 target players who stand either side of the goal (2 on each side).

The objective is to score with a header with an assist from a target player.

The game is played with the hands and heads.

Change target players.

---

## Practice 6  Free Small Sided Game     **20 mins**

---

# CHAPTER

## 7

# Receiving Training Unit

**Primary Technical objective:** Receiving the ball in the air and guided control.

**Coordination Objective:** Reading the trajectory of the ball and coordination abilities.

**Secondary Technical Objective:** Chipping and shooting.

**Tactical Objective:** 1v1s, creating space and 5v5s.

**Duration of Session:** 85-100 minutes

We recommend starting the session with exercises for general mobility to prevent injuries.

| Practice 1 | Juggling and Passing with 3 Players | 10 mins |

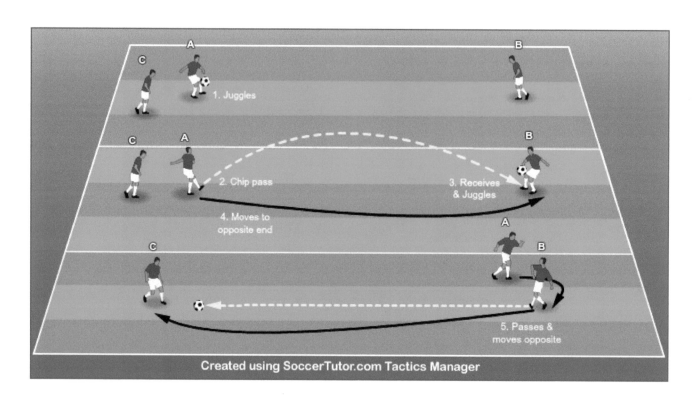

Created using SoccerTutor.com Tactics Manager

### Description

Player A juggles, chips the ball to player B, who controls the ball and passes to C. Player A follows his pass and takes up position B and Player B runs to take up Player A's starting position.

### Variation

Using only right foot or left foot.

### Coaching Points

1. If the game is too complex use the hands to pass the ball (throw).
2. Use all parts of the feet, thighs, chest and head to maximise control of the ball.

## Practice 2  Roll, Receive and Shoot

**10 mins**

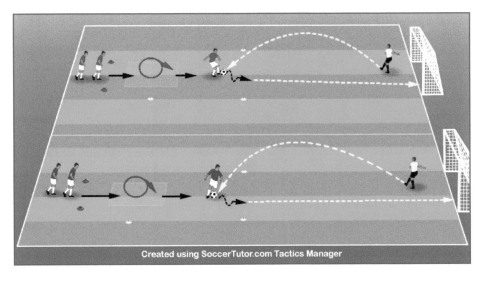

Created using SoccerTutor.com Tactics Manager

### Description

Every player does a forward roll and moves to receive the ball chipped by the goalkeeper.

Once the ball is controlled the can player shoots at goal.

The team with the most goals win the game.

### Variations

1.  The pass from the goalkeeper is along the ground.
2.  Receive the ball with a different part of the body.

### Coaching Point

1.  Receive the ball using a directional first touch to move forward and shoot at goal.

---

## Practice 3  Receiving with a Directional First Touch

**15-20 mins**

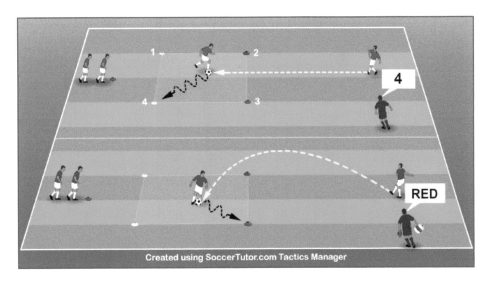

Created using SoccerTutor.com Tactics Manager

### Description

One player passes the ball into the square and the player inside must make a directional first touch to control the ball in the direction called by the coach (1,2,3 or 4).

We also use different parts of the foot when each number is called:

1.  Inside of foot and change direction.
2.  Inside of foot in a closed position.
3.  Inside of foot in an opened position.
4.  Outside of the foot and change direction.

### Variations

**1)** Use the weaker foot to receive. **2)** Chip pass. **3)** Use colours instead of numbers so the players have to be visually aware.

### Coaching Points

1.  Players should open up (half turned) to receive and change direction.
2.  The pass needs to be accurate and weighted well so the player has time to react and receive with different feet (and parts of the foot).

---

## Practice 4  Move, Receive and Score in a 1v1 Duel

**20 mins**

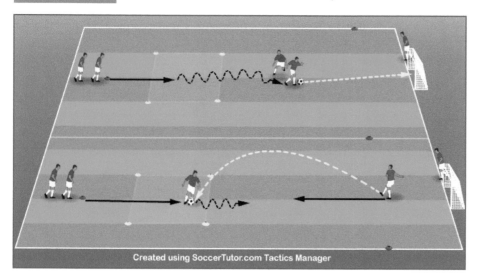

Created using SoccerTutor.com Tactics Manager

### Description

The first players sprint to the square and receive a pass from the opposing player at the other end.

The player receiving the pass has to quickly receive and shoot before the defender can tackle them (1v1 duel).

After 5 turns, switch the roles of the players.

### Variation

Pass and receive with the weaker foot.

### Coaching Points

1. Players should receive facing forwards, with a directional first touch out the front of the square.

2. Strength is needed to prevent the defending players from winning the ball (getting your body in between the opponent and the ball).

## Practice 5  Receiving in Corner Zones in a 7v7 SSG

**20 mins**

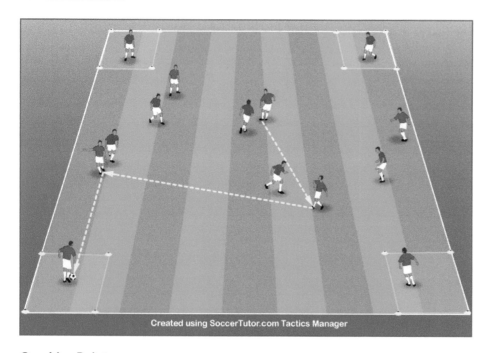

Created using SoccerTutor.com Tactics Manager

### Description

In an area 30 x 30 yards a game of 7v7 is played with each team having 1 player at each end in corner zones.

The objective of the game is to pass the ball to a teammates in one of the end zones. A goal is scored if this player controls the ball within the zone.

Once the player receives it in the end zone, he switches places with the player who made the pass and the game carries on.

### Coaching Points

1. Correct body shape (open up on the half turn) and positioning is important to view where the options for where the next pass is going.

2. Players need to quickly provide 2 options either side of the man in the corner to maintain possession.

## Practice 6  Free Small Sided Game

**20 mins**

SESSION 02

**Primary Technical objective:** Receiving the ball in the air.

**Coordination Objective:** Reading the trajectory of the ball, quickness and coordination abilities.

**Secondary Technical Objective:** Chipping, shooting, throw-ins and crossing.

**Tactical Objective:** 1v1s, creating space, attacking movements, covering of the goal and 5v5s.

**Duration of Session:** 85-100 minutes

We recommend starting the session with exercises for general mobility to prevent injuries.

---

**Practice 1**  Football Tennis with Coordination Exercises        **10 mins**

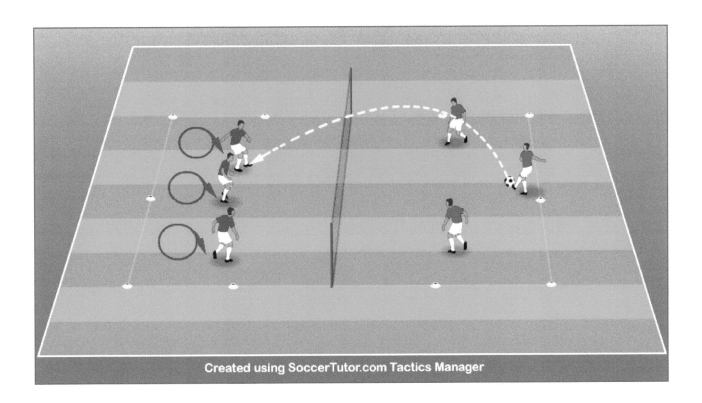

Created using SoccerTutor.com Tactics Manager

### Description

The team receiving the ball must perform a forward roll before controlling the ball chipped over by the other team. The rules of football tennis are applied.

Allow no bounces or 1 bounce and a minimum/maximum amount of touches depending on the age/level of the players.

### Variations

1. Side roll and receive.
2. Cartwheel and receive.
3. Dive and receive.

---

## Practice 2    Dribble, Cross Receive and Shoot     **10 mins**

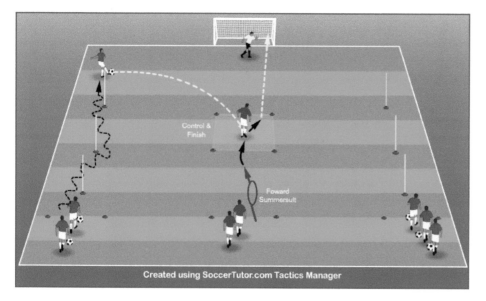

Created using SoccerTutor.com Tactics Manager

### Description

The red players dribble around the poles and cross the ball from near the touchline.

The blue players perform a roll and move to receive the ball in the square to shoot at goal.

Both feet must be used to cross the ball.

### Variations

**1)** Cartwheel and receive. **2)** Receive the ball and finish with a volley.

### Coaching Points

1. The first touch when receiving needs to push the ball out in front of the player to step onto and shoot.

2. Players need to use soft touches, keeping the ball close to their feet around the poles.

---

## Practice 3    Move, Receive and Volley     **15-20 mins**

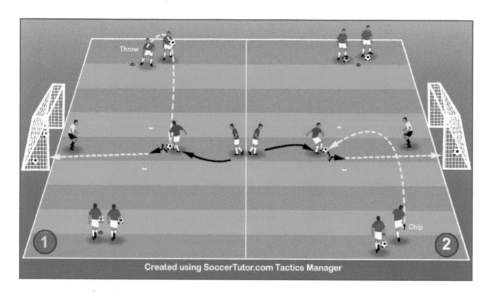

Created using SoccerTutor.com Tactics Manager

### Description

*GROUP 1*
The red players throw-in the ball to the blue players in the middle who control the ball and volley at goal (using 2 touches).

*GROUP 2*
The red players chip the ball to the blue players in the middle who control the ball and volley at goal (using 2 touches).

### Variations

1. Receive the ball with the chest, thigh, head or inside of the foot and volley.

2. Free control of the ball and half-volley.

## Practice 4 — Sprint, Receive and Score in a 1v1

**20 mins**

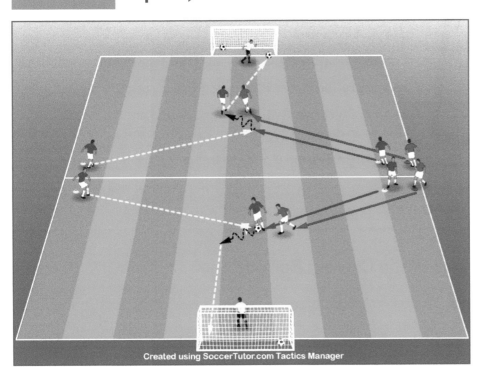

Created using SoccerTutor.com Tactics Manager

### Description

The blue players sprint to the middle and receive a pass from their teammate.

The red player tracks the run starting from a slight disadvantage.

The blue player has to quickly receive and shoot even though the defender is passive.

Run the drill from the left and the right.

### Variation

Make the defender active.

---

## Practice 5 — Switching Play with End Zones in a 7v7 SSG

**20-25 mins**

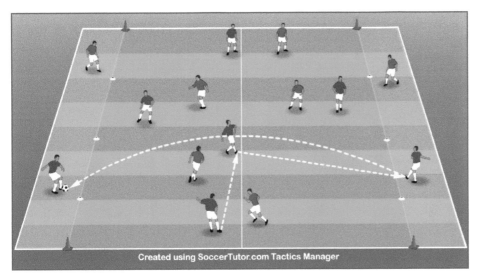

Created using SoccerTutor.com Tactics Manager

### Description

In an area 20 x 20 yards a game of 7v7 is played with each team having 1 player in each end zone.

The objective of the game is to work the ball to one of the teammates in an end zone and then switch it to the teammate in the other end zone using the players in the middle.

### Variation

The goal counts as double if the ball is chipped and controlled with the weaker foot.

### Coaching Points

1. The inside players need to be constantly thinking of changing the direction of play to the end zones.

2. Creating space and checking away before moving to receive will be essential to maintain possession and switch the play.

---

## Practice 6 — Free Small Sided Game

**20 mins**

---

**Primary Technical objective:** Receiving the ball on the ground and guided control.

**Coordination Objective:** Quickness and coordination abilities.

**Secondary Technical Objective:** Passing, shooting and dribbling.

**Tactical Objective:** 1v1s, creating space, marking, peripheral vision and defending the goal .

**Duration of Session:** 85-100 minutes

We recommend starting the session with exercises for general mobility to prevent injuries.

---

| Practice 1 | Receiving with the Correct Body Shape | 10 mins |

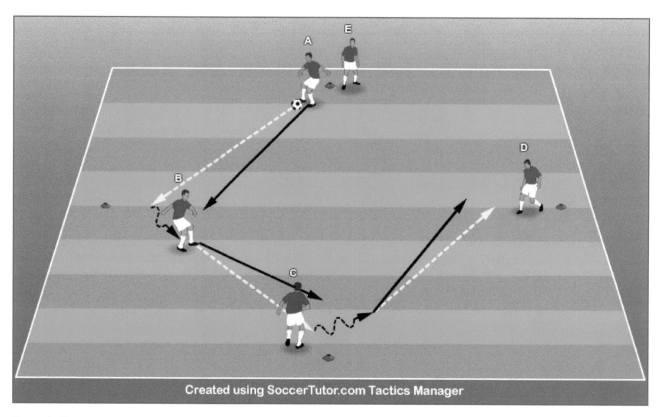

Created using SoccerTutor.com Tactics Manager

## Description

Player A passes to B and follows the pass. Player B receives by opening up with the inside of the right foot, moves around player A and passes to player c.

The exercise is run in an anti-clockwise direction. The players with the most correct controls (determined by the coach) win the game.

## Variation

Play in a clockwise direction, receiving with the inside of the left foot.

## Coaching Points

1. Players should receive and pass with the back foot.

2. They should already be half turned when receiving, letting the ball roll across their body.

3. A directional first touch is needed for a smoother transition to the pass.

---

**Practice 2** | **Coordination, Passing and Receiving Game** | **10 mins**

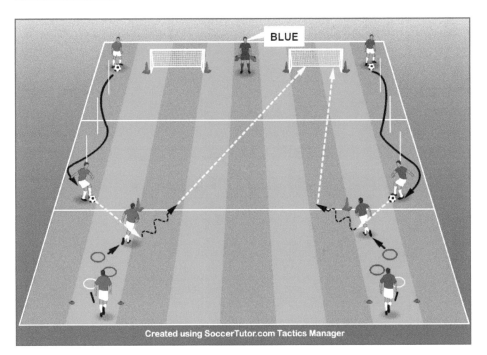

Created using SoccerTutor.com Tactics Manager

### Description

2 players start at the same time with the ball, dribble through the poles and pass to their teammate who has skipped through the rings.

The coach calls the goal which the players must shoot in.

A point is won for the team by the player who scores first.

### Variation

Change the positioning of the rings and poles.

---

**Practice 3** | **Opening Up to Receive and Dribble** | **15-20 mins**

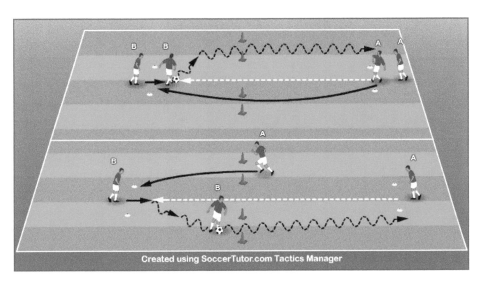

Created using SoccerTutor.com Tactics Manager

### Description

Player A passes the ball to player B. Player B receives the ball and takes a directional first touch to either the left or right and then dribbles through the cones to the other end and gives the ball to the next player.

The Player A who made the first pass runs through the opposite cones to move to the opposite end (as shown).

### Variation

Use a chip pass.

### Coaching Points

1. Players should pass and receive with both feet during this practice.

2. The dribbling part should be done at full speed.

## Practice 4    Receive the Ball and Score in a 2v1    20 mins

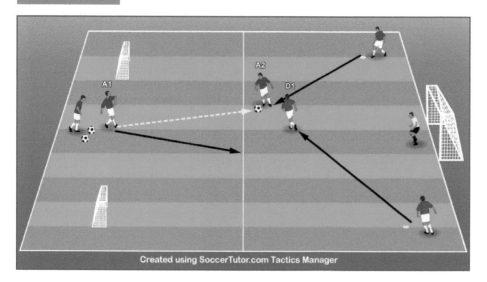

Created using SoccerTutor.com Tactics Manager

### Description

Player A1 passes to A2 who is closed down by D1.

A2 receives the ball and is joined by A1 as they try to score in a 2v1 situation.

If the defender wins the ball, they can score in one of the 2 small goals.

### Variations

**1)** Chip pass. **2)** Pass with the weaker foot. **3)** introduce another defender for a 2v2.

### Coaching Points

1. Receive the ball making sure to make the body a barrier between the ball and the defender (shielding).

2. Decision making is important; when to hold the ball, play a first time pass or dribble forwards.

## Practice 5    Creating Space to Receive in a 7v7 Game    20-25 mins

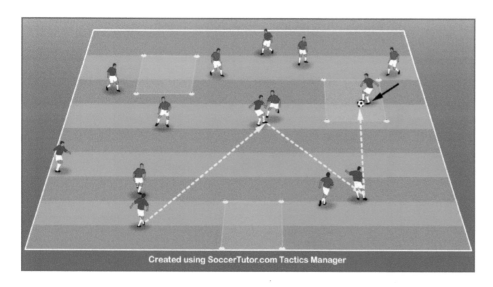

Created using SoccerTutor.com Tactics Manager

### Description

A game of 7v7 is played in an area 35 x 35 yards with 3 squares 4 x 4 yards.

A goal is scored when a player successfully receives the ball in one of the squares free of any marking.

The defending team are not allowed to enter the squares.

### Variation

Increase the number of the boxes.

### Coaching Points

1. Correct body shape (open up on the half turn) and positioning is important to view where the options for where the next pass is going.

2. Checking away from the marker before moving to receive will be essential to creating space.

## Practice 6    Free Small Sided Game    20 mins

**Primary Technical objective:** Receiving the ball on the ground and guided control.

**Coordination Objective:** Quickness and coordination abilities.

**Secondary Technical Objective:** Passing, shooting and dribbling.

**Tactical Objective:** 1v1s, creating space, marking, peripheral vision and defending the goal.

**Duration of Session:** 85-100 minutes

We recommend starting the session with exercises for general mobility to prevent injuries.

---

| Practice 1 | Receiving with Back to Goal - Turn and Shoot | 10 mins |

Created using SoccerTutor.com Tactics Manager

### Description

The player with the ball passes into the square to the other player who receives, takes a directional first touch to turn and then shoots at goal.

This drill should be run from both sides so players use both feet.

### Variation

Receiving with the inside of the foot or the outside of the foot.

### Coaching Points

1. Players should receive the ball on the half turn with a directional first touch setting up to shoot.

2. Receive the ball with the back foot and an open body shape.

---

## Practice 2 — Quick Reactions - Receive, Dribble and Shoot  **10 mins**

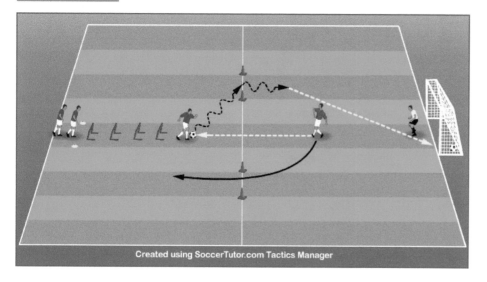

### Description

Here the red player tests the reactions of the blue player.

The blue player jumps over the hurdles, receives the ball passed by the red player and dribbles the ball through the cones (left or right) opposite to where the red player runs.

Once the blue player dribbles through the cones, they can shoot at goal.

### Variations

1. Receiving the ball with the inside or outside of the foot.
2. Frontal jump or sideways jump over hurdles.

## Practice 3 — Passing and Receiving Around a Pole  **15-20 mins**

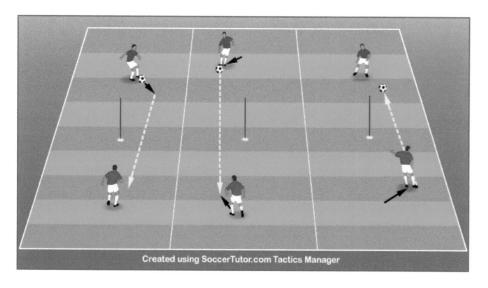

### Description

Players are in pairs and pass the ball to each other with a pole in between them.

The players can move closer and further away from each other.

A maximum of 2 touches are used to receive and pass.

### Variations

1. Pass with the inside of the right foot and receive with the inside of the left foot.
2. Pass with inside left and receive with inside right.
3. Pass with inside right and receive with outside right.
4. Pass with inside left and receive with left.

## Practice 4   Receive the Ball and Score in a 2v1 (2)     20 mins

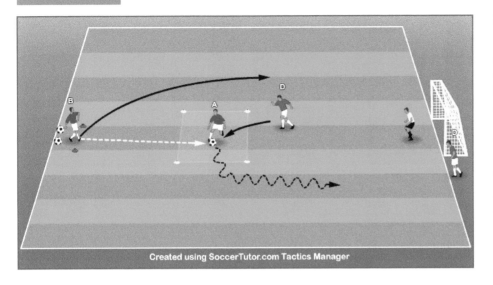

### Description

Player B passes to player A inside the square. Player A must make a counter movement to create space and receive the ball. Player B must run in the opposite direction to where player A runs with the ball.

The players compete in a 2v1 trying to score a goal against active defender (D) and the keeper.

### Variation

Ask the players to use the various parts of the foot to receive the ball.

### Coaching Points

1. Receive the ball making sure to make the body a barrier between the ball and the defender (shielding).
2. Decision making is important; when to hold the ball, play a first time pass or dribble forwards.

---

## Practice 5   8v8 Game with 2 Sided Goals & Striker Zones    20-25 mins

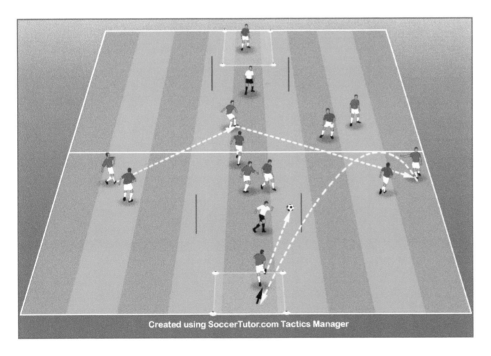

### Description

In an area 30 x 30 yards we play a game of 7v7.

Goals can be scored on both sides of the goals. 2 squares are made at each end which are 5 x 5 yards placed 10 yards from the goal line.

If a goal is scored by passing to the attacker in the box and finished with 1 touch it counts double.

### Variations

1. Chip the ball to the player in the square.
2. After 5 passes the player in the square can play with 2 touches.

---

## Practice 6   Free Small Sided Game        20 mins

---

**Primary Technical objective:** Receiving the ball on the ground and guided control.

**Coordination Objective:** Quickness and coordination abilities.

**Secondary Technical Objective:** Passing, shooting and dribbling.

**Tactical Objective:** 1v1s, creating space, marking, anticipation and defending the goal.

**Duration of Session:** 85-100 minutes

We recommend starting the session with exercises for general mobility to prevent injuries.

---

| Practice 1 | Receiving, Dribbling & 1v1 with a Goalkeeper | 10 mins |

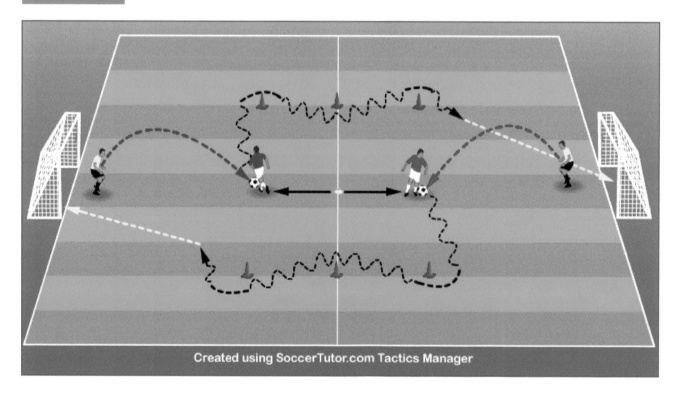

Created using SoccerTutor.com Tactics Manager

### Description

The goalkeepers pass the ball to the players in the middle who move forward, control the ball, then dribble around the cones as shown in the diagram and shoot at goal.

### Variations

1. Receiving the ball with the inside or outside of the foot.
2. Have the pass from the goalkeeper low and driven.

### Coaching Points

1. Receive the ball with a directional first touch to start dribbling in one movement.
2. Players need to use soft touches, keeping the ball close to their feet around the cones.

## Practice 2 | Agility & Quickness in a 1v1 Shooting Game | 10 mins

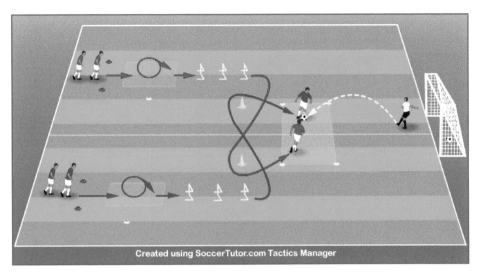

Created using SoccerTutor.com Tactics Manager

### Description

Players perform a cartwheel then jump over the hurdles at maximum speed.

The first player to the ball chipped by the goalkeeper into the area receives and shoots at goal while the other player defends.

### Variation

Forward roll, frontal jumping or sideways jumping.

### Coaching Point

1. Players need to demonstrate great balance and coordination to complete all the different parts of this exercise well.

## Practice 3 | Receiving on the Move and Guided Control | 15-20 mins

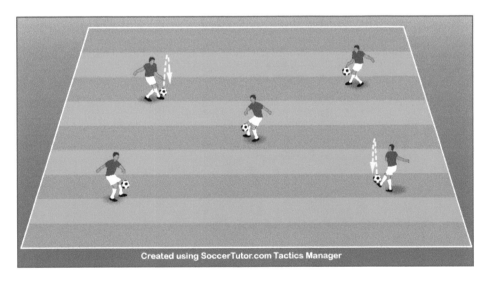

Created using SoccerTutor.com Tactics Manager

### Description

Every player has a ball.

Every 3 touches while juggling, the player kicks the ball in the air and then receives with a guided control.

### Variations

1. Receiving with the right or left instep.
2. Receive the ball with the inside of the foot and move into space.
3. Receive with the outside of the right or left foot and move into space.
4. Receive with the sole of the foot and move the ball into space.
5. Receive with chest and inside of foot and move into space.

## Practice 4 — Receive the Ball and Dribble Under Pressure — 20 mins

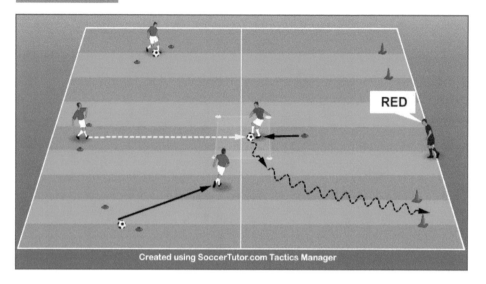

### Description

The red player passes the ball into the square and the other red player applies pressure.

The blue player receives the ball and scores a goal if he can dribble the ball through the coloured cones called out by the coach (red or blue).

### Variation

Players have to use inside of foot, outside of foot, left or right, when receiving the ball.

## Practice 5 — 7v7 Game with 4 Goals - 'Receive from Behind' — 20-25 mins

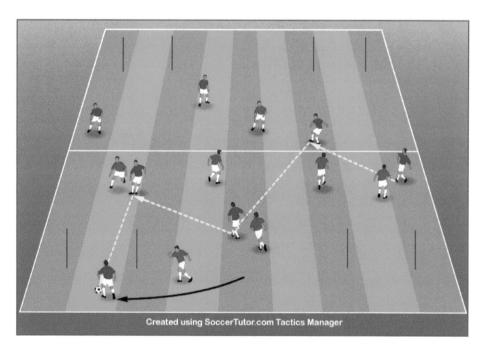

### Description

We play a 7v7 game in an area 30 x 30 yards with 4 goals.

A goal is scored when a player successfully receives the ball behind one of the goals.

### Variation

Game with limited touches.

### Coaching Points

1. Players need to check away from their marker before moving to receive (creating space).
2. 1 touch passing should be used when possible to speed up play.

## Practice 6 — Free Small Sided Game — 20 mins

# CHAPTER

## 8

# Juggling Training Unit

**Primary Technical objective:** Ball control (juggling).

**Coordination Objective:** Reading the trajectory, quickness and coordination abilities.

**Secondary Technical Objective:** Chip passing, shooting and receiving.

**Tactical Objective:** Creating Space.

**Duration of Session:** 85-100 minutes

We recommend starting the session with exercises for general mobility to prevent injuries.

---

**Practice 1**  **Juggling Around Poles with 3 Players**  **10 mins**

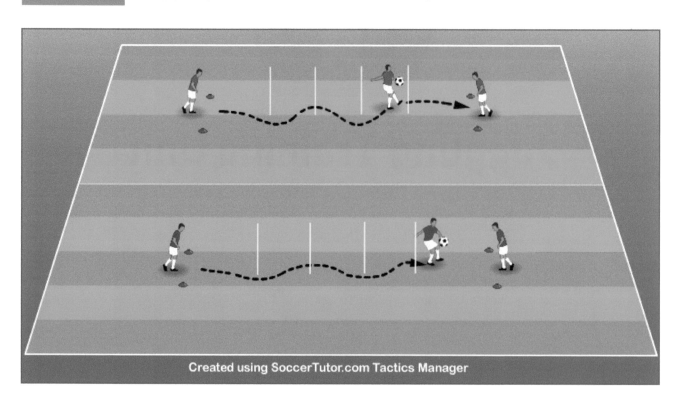

Created using SoccerTutor.com Tactics Manager

### Description

A point is scored if a player can juggle the ball through the poles to the player on the other side without the ball hitting the ground.

The players work in groups of 3.

### Variations

1. Juggling only with only the right or left foot.
2. Juggling with the thigh or juggling with just the head.

### Coaching Points

1. Players should use both feet to juggle round the poles to maximise their control of the ball.
2. Soft touches are needed to keep close control of the ball to the feet.

---

## Practice 2   Juggling with Obstacles and Shooting    10 mins

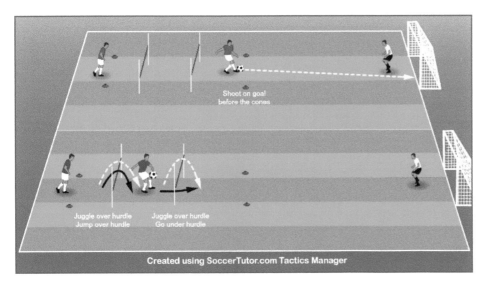

### Description

Players must juggle through these obstacles with 1 player from each team starting at the same time.

At the first obstacle, the player must juggle the ball over it and jump over it.

At the second obstacle, the player must juggle over it and go under it.

The exercise ends with a shot on goal. Whoever scores first gets the point for their team.

### Variation

Juggling only with the right or left foot.

### Coaching Point

1. Kick the ball high up in the air to allow time to jump over the obstacle and then control the ball.

## Practice 3   Juggling Through Obstacles and Shooting    15-20 mins

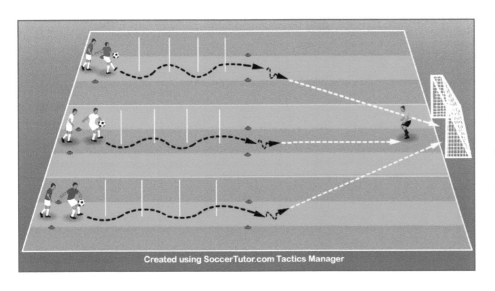

### Description

Players juggle through the poles maintaining control of the ball.

They then must juggle through the cones and shoot at goal.

We have 3 players starting at the same time and the first 2 players to score get a point for their team.

### Variations

1. Juggling only with right or left foot.

2. Juggling only with the thigh.

3. Volley or acrobatic shot at the end.

## Practice 4  Juggling and Shooting vs Goalkeeper

**20 mins**

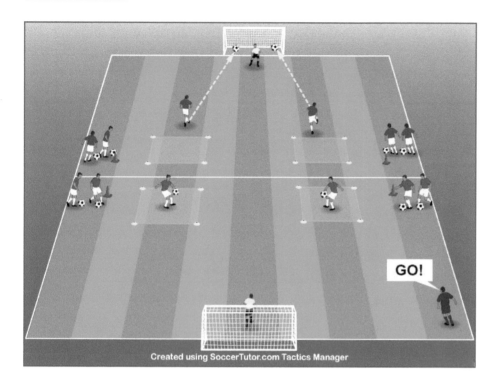

Created using SoccerTutor.com Tactics Manager

### Description

The players inside the square must juggle with 5 touches before they can shoot at goal.

The team with the most goals in the allocated time win.

### Variations

1. Juggling only with right or left foot.
2. Juggling only with the thigh.
3. Acrobatic shot.
4. Control and dribbling for a 1v1 with the GK.

## Practice 5  5v5 Juggling Small Sided Game

**25 mins**

Created using SoccerTutor.com Tactics Manager

### Description

We play a 4v4 game with the aim to build up play using only juggling.

The team without possession cannot tackle the players from the other team but can intercept the ball when it is passed in the air.

the ball hits the ground, possession is given to the other team.

### Variation

2 points for a goal with an acrobatic shot or only allow headed goals.

### Coaching Points

1. Make sure the passes have good height, making it easier to control and maintain possession.
2. Use all parts of the feet, thighs, chest and head to maximise control of the ball.

## Practice 6  Free Small Sided Game

**20 mins**

# CHAPTER

## 9

# Throw-Ins Training Unit

**Primary Technical objective:** Throw-ins.

**Coordination Objective:** Quickness, motor skills, coordination abilities and reading the trajectory of the ball.

**Secondary Technical Objective:** Receiving, shooting and running with the ball.

**Tactical Objective:** 1v1 marking, defending the goal and 4v4s.

**Duration of Session:** 85-100 minutes

We recommend starting the session with exercises for general mobility to prevent injuries.

---

| Practice 1 | Throw-ins Accuracy - 'Hit the Target' | 10 mins |

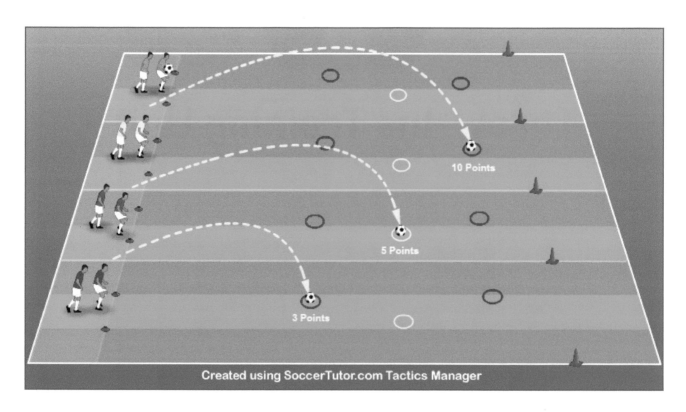

Created using SoccerTutor.com Tactics Manager

### Description

2 teams compete to hit the rings by throwing the ball using the proper throw-in technique.

Assign various points to the rings based on difficulty and/or distance.

### Variation

Change the type of throw.

---

## Practice 2   Speed & Agility Circuit with Throw-ins    10 mins

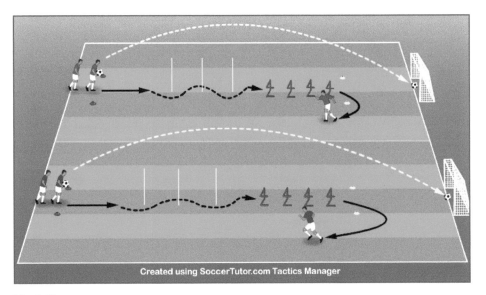

### Description

Each player in the team has a ball and they try to score in the goal with a throw-in.

After the throw they run around the poles, jump over the hurdles and then run to the back of the line.

The team that scores the most goals in a minute wins a point.

### Variation

Change the type of throw.

### Coaching Points

1. Monitor the correct technique for the long throw.
2. Players should use quick side-to-side steps when running through the poles.

## Practice 3   Throw-in Accuracy - 'Hit the Ball in the Air'    15-20 mins

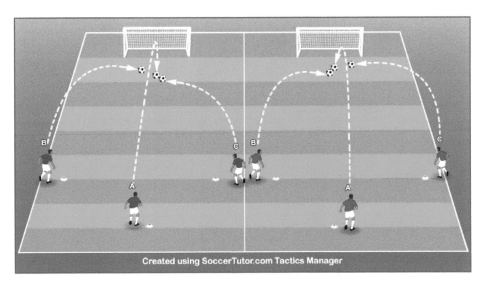

### Description

Groups of 3 players play this throw-in practice.

Player A throws the ball in the air, then players B and C try to hit the ball with their ball.

Players must use the proper throw-in technique.

Points are scored when they hit the ball

### Variation

Throw with 1 hand or throw-in with 1 foot in front of the other.

## Practice 4 | Throw-in, Receive and 1v1 Duel

**20 mins**

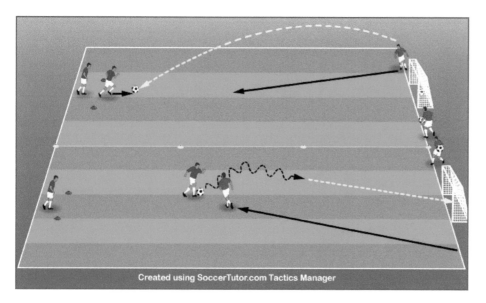

Created using SoccerTutor.com Tactics Manager

### Description

The player standing beside the goal throws the ball to the attacker who receives and a 1v1 situation begins.

The attacker tries to score in the small goal and the red defender tries to stop a goal being scored.

### Variation

Throw with 1 hand or throw-in with 1 foot in front of the other.

### Coaching Points

1. Monitor the correct technique for the long throw.
2. Players need to be strong in their 1v1 situations (shield the ball from the opponent).

## Practice 5 | Hands and Feet Small Sided Game

**25 mins**

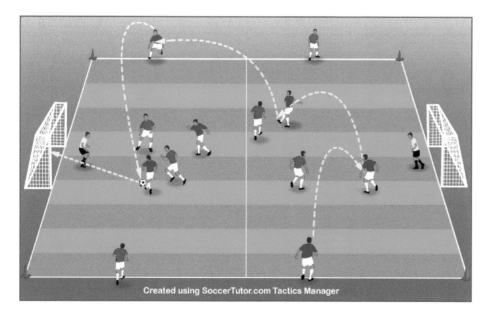

Created using SoccerTutor.com Tactics Manager

### Description

We play a game of 7v7 with 4 outside players in an area 20 x 20 yards.

Inside the area, the rule is that a pass with the hands is followed by a pass with the feet.

When the ball is played to the outside players they must use a throw-in to pass the ball back inside the pitch.

### Variation

Inside the area players play with their feet and the outside players play with their hands.

## Practice 6 | Free Small Sided Game

**20 mins**

# CHAPTER
## 10

# Motor Activity For 9 to 12 Year Old Players

# Motor Activity For 9 to 12 Year Old Players

Coaches and athletic trainers who work in youth sport environments are obligated to know the characteristics of the body in every age level, in order to facilitate the planning of activities that are balanced and effective and guarantee the harmonious growth of the player.

The main objective of the youth sport preparation is a general development of the motor skills in a framework of education and global formation of the personality, respecting the laws that control the physiological and psychological formation.

For this reason it is necessary to work on the basic formation of the motor skills, aimed to a general harmonious development of the body.

Between the ages of 9 and 12, for which we have experimented the following exercises, there is an overlapping of the initial sport specialisation and the introductory activity of the previous years.

The game is still used as a fun activity a lot in the training sessions because it is a requirement for this age level.

Especially in younger players and still in this age level we must devote some time to the consolidation and the coordination of the motor skills and the coordination abilities.

The twelfth year is usually the finishing point for the 'functional pre-requisites'. In training sessions we keep working on exercises of a general nature compared to those of a more specific nature, even though the percentage of time devoted to the latter is considerably increased.

From and athletic point of view we keep working on the abilities of the previous phase, with a higher workloadbut not at maximum levels.

We will not work as yet on specific exercises for the development of the anaerobic endurance and of the maximal strength.

Therefore it is important to avoid training methods that produce the accumulation of lactic acid in the blood, as well as weights or isometric gymnastics.

The **only conditional abilities that we can work on are** the **aerobic endurance** (preferably with the use of games with the ball), the quick strength (with a methodology that does not involve excessiveworkloads), **speed**, **quickness** and all the exercises of **mobility** and **flexibility** together with **stretching** exercises.

Fast runs with quick change of direction, relay runs with various starting situations are the methods we use to work on quickness and reaction ability.

It is important to allow recovery time between repetitions (not too intense but also not too limited) to allow the performance of all the activities to be at the appropriate intensity.

# Coordination Abilities

The coordination abilities allow the execution of a movement as close as possible to the mental solution of the problem after analysing a situation.

We can also define the abilities and the processes of organisation, control and regulation of the movement.

They are based on the assumption and the elaboration of information coming from the outside and the inside of someone's body (perceptions) and the possibility to execute and adapt the movement based on the pattern chosen.

The coordination abilities are the fundamental pre-requisite for the learning and development of motor skills and consequently to form a good technical level.

The more the athletes will reach a high level of coordination abilities, the less difficulty it will be to learn new or more complex movements.

The coordination abilities are important because they determine the accuracy and the control of the movement and therefore the management of energy consumption during the execution of the motor gesture.

Each ability has a sensitive phase in each age level, when it can be improved the most. These phases are limited to the period of time when children mature (puberty) where there is a more intense reaction to the stimulus introduced in training, both from a psychologically and physiologically point of view.

Nonetheless, there is still much room for improvement outside of these sensitive phases.

# Technical Fundamental And Associated Coordination Ability

| Technical Fundamental | Associated Coordination ability |
|---|---|
| | |
| Passing | Balance – Adaptation, Transformation and Differentiation |
| Running with the Ball | Rhythm – Motor Combinations and Orientation |
| Shooting | Differentiation – Balance - Reactions |
| Receiving the Ball | Differentiation and Motor Combinations |
| Heading | Rhythm – Adaptation and Transformation |
| Throw-ins | Differentiation |
| Juggling | Balance – Adaptation, Transformation and Differentiation |

# CHAPTER

## 11

# Training Sessions With Specific Motor Coordination Exercises

# Coordination Required For Technical Training

The coordination abilities that we will study in this book, with specific exercises, are the following:

## Space and Time Orientation

The ability to define and vary the position and the body movements in space and in time in the context of space available on the pitch.

## Balance

Ability to maintain balance both in a static form and dynamic form.

## Motor combination

The ability to combine movements of different body parts, various motor gestures and various technical abilities.

## Adaptation and transformation

The ability of an individual, while performing an action and based on the variations perceived or derived from a situation, to adapt and change the planned course of action and execute a different action.

## Reactions

The ability to perform a movement or modify it in the quickest possible way in relation to a visual, audio and tactile stimulus, taking into consideration the technical fundamentals.

## Differentiation

The ability to apply the appropriate muscular tension depending on the motor requirement.

## Rhythm

The ability to give a specific chronological order to a motor gesture.

# Differentiation

**Practice 1**   Ball Touches with Varied Distancess

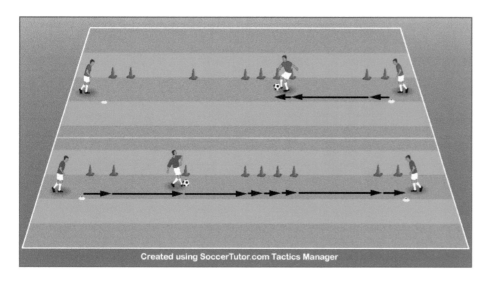

Created using SoccerTutor.com Tactics Manager

### Description

We have a circuit with cones placed at various distances from each other.

The players have to roll the ball from one cone to the next using different weighted touches to adapt to the different distances between the cones.

### Variation

Vary the distances of the cones and change the part of the foot to touch the ball with.

---

**Practice 2**   Passing & Receiving in Zones with Changing Distances

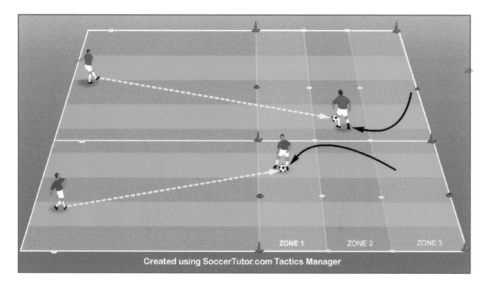

ZONE 1      ZONE 2      ZONE 3

Created using SoccerTutor.com Tactics Manager

### Description

The first player passes to their teammate positioned in one of the 3 zones.

After each pass, the player receiving the ball changes zone and waits for the next pass.

The player making the pass must use the correct weight based on the zone where the player is positioned.

### Variations

1. Pass on the ground.
2. Chip pass.
3. Pass with the hands.

## Practice 3 — Aerial Passing and Receiving

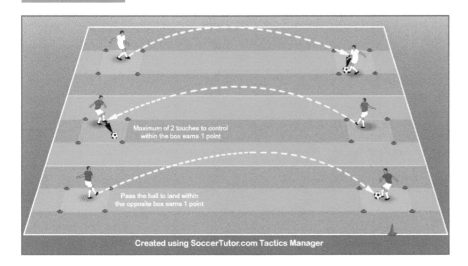

### Description

In this practice 2 players exchange chipped passes, receiving in their squares. The player receiving uses a maximum of 2 touches control the ball and chip pass it back to the other square.

If a player misses the square with the pass or is unable to control a ball that lands in the square, their opponent wins 1 point.

## Practice 4 — Weight of the Pass & Vision - 'Coloured Boxes'

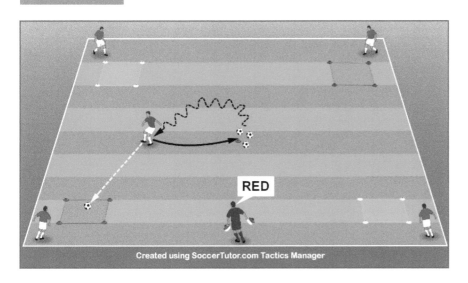

### Description

The player runs with the ball and on the coach's call, passes into one of the squares.

The ball has to stay within the square to score a point.

Use balls of different size and weight.

You can use visual signals to determine which colour square to pass into.

## Practice 5 — Accurate Finishing with Visual Awareness

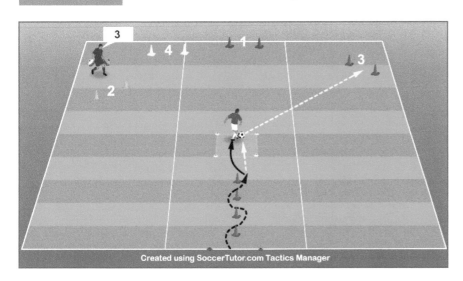

### Description

The player dribbles around the cones, passes to himself inside the square and then passes through the cones called out by the coach.

The goals must be placed at different distances to work on the accuracy and weight of passing.

You can use visual signals to determine which colour goal.

# Reactions

| Practice 1 | **Agility, Vision and Quick Reactions Exercise** |

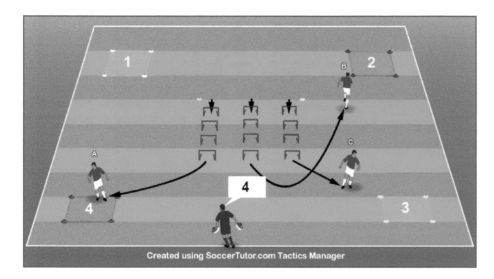

**Description**

Assign a number to each square. The players jump over the low hurdles and then wait for a number to be called for player A to go to that square.

At the same time, player B must run to the diagonally opposite cone and player C in any of the 2 other squares.

**Variations**

1. Change the hurdle section: Low jump, high jump, forward roll, backwards run or run with the ball.

2. Change the second phase of the exercise:
   Modify the sequence of the players, use visual signs to determine the squares, call the number using maths equations (i.e 2+1 and player A will have to go to cone 3) or without calling the number (player A will decide where to go).

---

| Practice 2 | **Passing & Receiving in Zones with Changing Distances** |

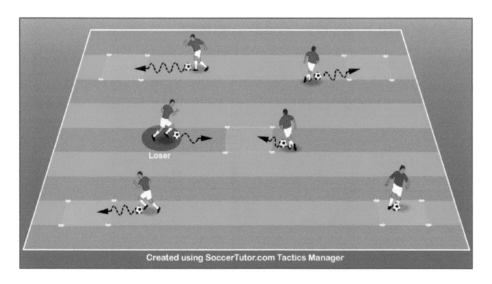

**Description**

Players run freely with the ball.

When the blue player stops the ball in 1 of the squares, the other players must quickly run with the ball to any other square.

The is 1 less square than player so 1 player loses as he will be without a square.

**Variations**

1. Pass on the ground.

2. Chip pass.

3. Play with the hands.

## Practice 3    Changing the Direction of Attack in a Small Sided Game

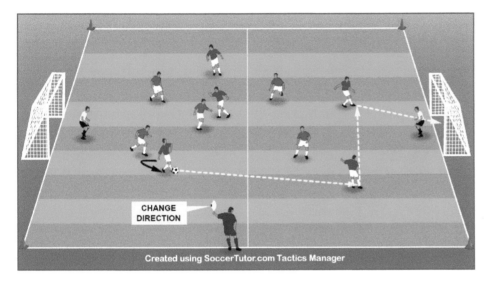

### Description

A normal small sided game is played.

However, on the coach's whistle the teams change the direction of play without stopping and have to attack the opposite goal.

### Variation

Substitute the whistle with visual signs (as shown by the yellow cone in the diagram).

## Practice 4    Exploiting a Numerical Advantage in a 3v2 Situation

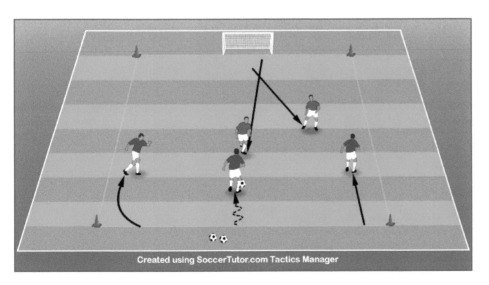

### Description

The central player dribbles the ball forward and the more advanced defender applies passive pressure.

At the same time the other defender decides to close down 1 of the other 2 attackers.

The player with the ball will have to pass the ball to the player who is not marked and they try to score with a 3v2.

## Practice 5  Vision and Awareness Passing Sequence Practice

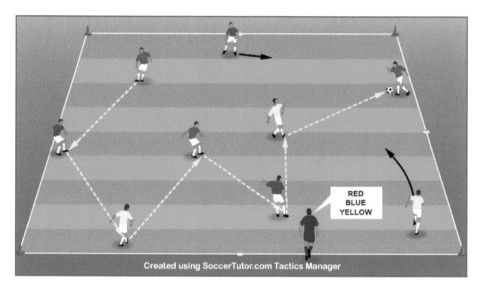

RED
BLUE
YELLOW

Created using SoccerTutor.com Tactics Manager

### Description

Players pass the ball around the area in the colour sequence established by the coach.

In the diagram the coach has called out Red, Blue, Yellow.

The players have to pass to each other using that exact sequence (as shown).

### Variations

1. Change the sequence of colours often.

2. Limit the players to a maximum amount of touches and require them to pass with a specific part of the foot.

## Practice 6  6v3 Dynamic Possession Game

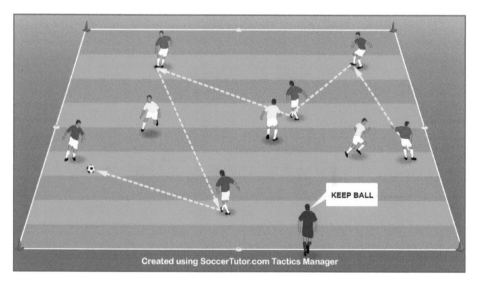

KEEP BALL

Created using SoccerTutor.com Tactics Manager

### Description

Passing between the different colours again and the players start by passing around freely.

On the coach's whistle, the team in possession joins with the team that made the last pass and they play possession football against the other team who must try to win the ball.

# Adaptation and Transformation

**Dribbling and Passing Alley**

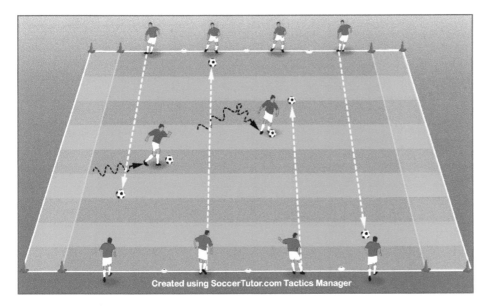

### Description

Players are in pairs 10 yards apart.

They pass the ball back and forth to each other.

The blue players dribble the ball through the channel formed by the pairs of players and try to avoid being hit by the ball, changing direction and using moves/feints.

**Variation**

Modify the types of passes.

---

**Creating 2 Passing Options in a Square**

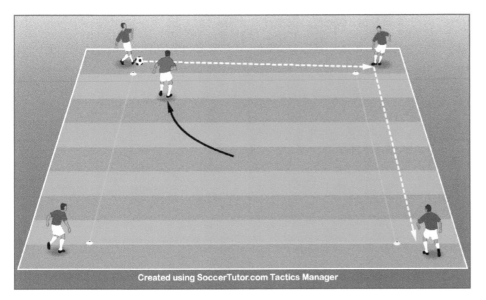

### Description

The 4 blue players must pass the ball to each other while they stand on the corners of the square and they move in such a way that the player in possession always has 2 options to pass the ball.

The red player applies passive pressure to the player with the ball.

Change the defender every 2 minutes.

## Practice 3   Dribbling and Passing Gates in a Small Sided Game

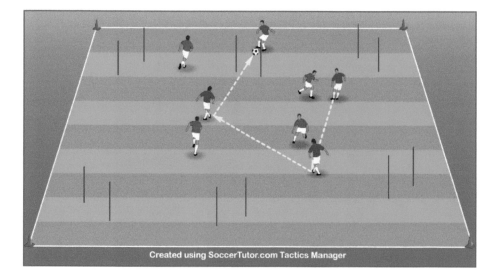

### Description

We have a game between 2 teams. Place small gates on the field (2 more than the players in each team (diagram is 4v4 game with 6 gates).

A goal can be scored in various ways:

1. By dribbling through the gates.
2. By receiving the ball on the other side of the gate.
3. They can score 1 point after 3 completed passes between different players.

## Practice 4   Psycho-Kinetics with 4 Coloured Goals in a SSG

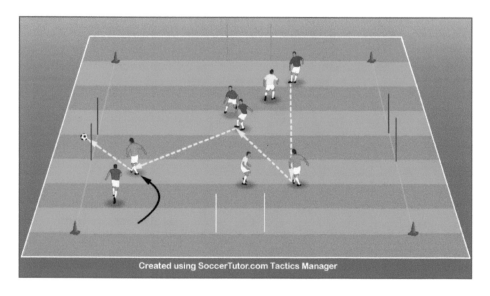

### Description

Here we have a game between 4 teams. Each goal has a colour of one of the teams.

Form alliances between teams, for example 2 teams vs 2 teams.

The players with the same colour cannot pass the ball to each other. A goal can only be scored in the goal with the colour of the opposition.

Change the alliances during the game.

## Practice 5  Crossing from the Flank with 1v1 Zones in the Centre

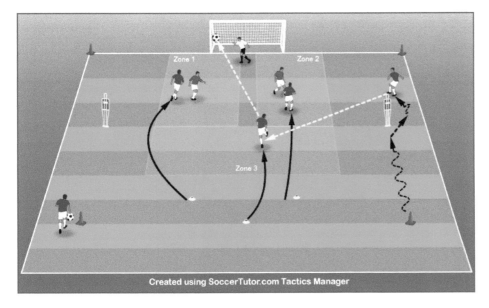

### Description

The player runs with the ball to the mannequin, makes a feint round it and then passes to the teammate free from the defender.

Zone 1 is a cross on the far post, zone 2 is a cross to the near post and zone 3 is a pass back along the ground.

The 2 defenders apply passive pressure on the 2 attackers in zones 1 and 2.

## Practice 6  Ball Control Obstacle Circuit

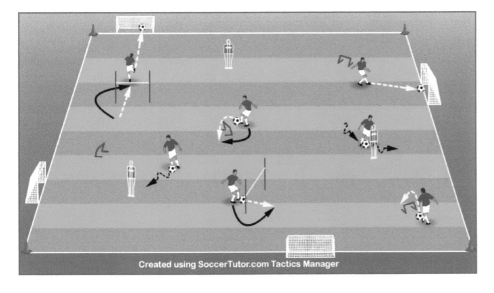

### Description

The players run with the ball with various obstacles placed on the ground.

The player must adapt their ball control and dribbling techniques for the various obstacles.

Mannequins: Perform a feint or change of direction.

Hurdles: The ball must be juggled over them.

High obstacles: The ball is passed underneath.

Goal: The player must shoot in it.

# Space and Time Orientation

---

**Practice 1**   'Creating Shapes Together' Vision & Awareness Practice

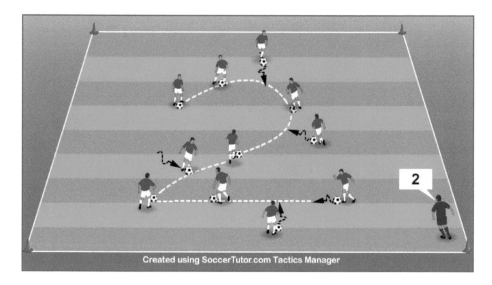

Created using SoccerTutor.com Tactics Manager

### Description

Players dribble the ball freely around a square.

The coach calls out a number and the players must group together to form the corresponding geometric shape.

The diagram shows the players moving to form the shape of the number 2.

---

**Practice 2**   Passing in Between Players

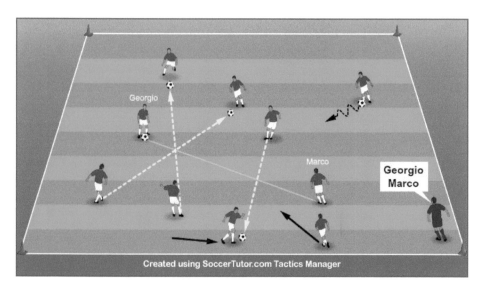

Georgio

Marco

Georgio
Marco

Created using SoccerTutor.com Tactics Manager

### Description

Players dribble the ball freely.

They wait for the coach who calls 2 players by name who must stand still.

The other players must position themselves on either side of an imaginary line passing between the players called.

### Variation

The coach calls more players by name who must form an imaginary geometric shape and the remainder of the players can position themselves inside or outside of the shape.

---

## Practice 3 'Knock the Cones Down' Small Side Game

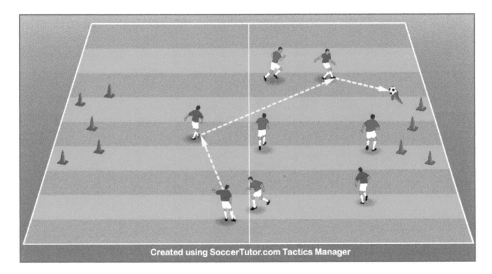

### Description

A game is played between 2 teams and the players must hit the cones to score.

Every time a cone is hit the player removes it from the pitch.

The blue players aim to hit the red cones and viceversa.

## Practice 4 5v4 Dynamic Possession Game

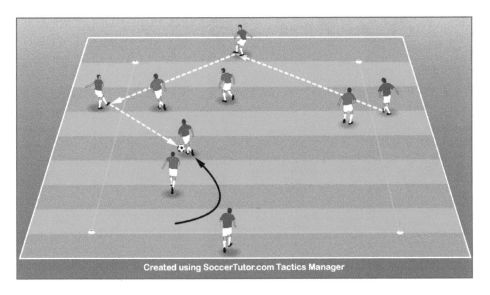

### Description

Blue players are outside of the square and the red players are inside together with 1 blue player.

The blue players have possession of the ball and must aim to pass the ball to their player inside the square.

A point is scored every time the ball is passed to the inside player.

## Practice 5 — Dynamic Possession Game with 4 Goals

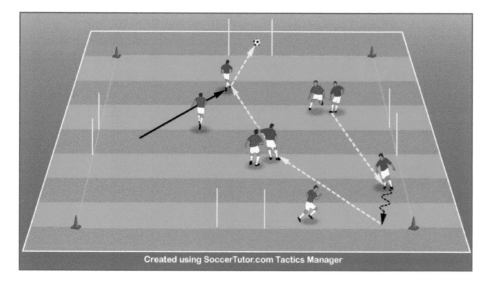

Created using SoccerTutor.com Tactics Manager

### Description

Here we have a game with 4 goals.

1 point is scored after a predetermined number of passes are completed.

2 points are scored every time that the ball is carried to the corner of the square.

3 points are scored every time a goal is scored in any of the 4 goals.

## Practice 6 — Quick Reactions Heading and Passing Practice

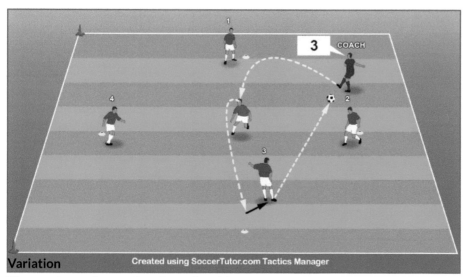

Created using SoccerTutor.com Tactics Manager

**Variation**

The coach can change the players' positions.

### Description

4 players form a diamond shape and each of them is assigned a number.

The player in the middle (red) waits for the coach to chip the ball in and he must head the ball passed by the coach to the player with the number the coach calls out.

The blue players receive, control the ball and pass back to the coach.

Change the inside player every 2 minutes.

# Rhythm

Practice 1 ## Changing the Rhythm of Play in a 3 Zone SSG

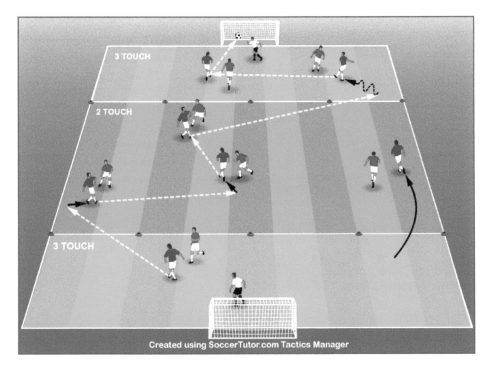

**Description**

Here we have a 3 zone game with an emphasis on changing the rhythm of play.

In the end zones, players play with 3 touches and in the middle zone the players play with 1 or 2 touches.

Practice 2 ## Ball Control with Cones at Varying Distances

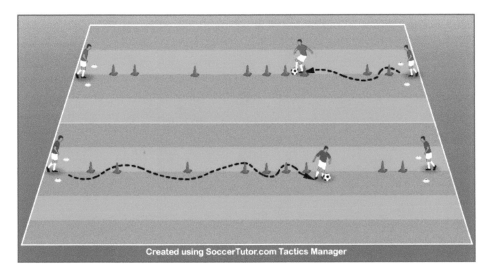

**Description**

Here we have a circuit with variations of rhythm to be performed with the ball or without going through the cones (as shown in the diagram).

The distance between the cones varies therefore the weight of the touches on the ball varies.

## Practice 3　Ball Control 'Touch the Ball on the Whistle'

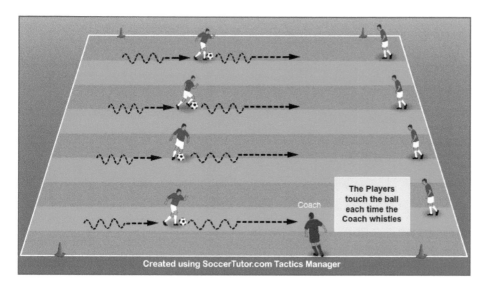

Coach

The Players touch the ball each time the Coach whistles

Created using SoccerTutor.com Tactics Manager

### Description

Players run with the ball and must take a touch on the ball each time the coach blows the whistle.

Players have to stop, start and take quick touches depending on the coach and have to constantly change the rhythm of their dribbling.

### Variations

1.  Change the type of dribbling.
2.  Juggle instead of dribble the ball.

# Motor Combinations

## Practice 1    Control, Pass, Skip and Receive

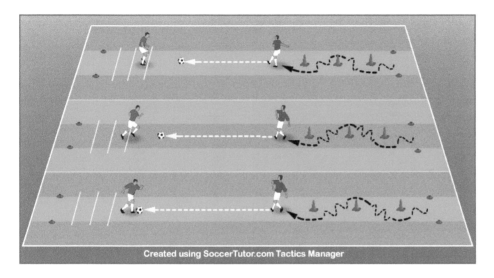

**Description**

The blue player runs with the ball through the cones as shown and then passes to the red player.

The red player has skipped over the poles laid on the ground and moves forward to receive the pass.

Players change position after each pass.

## Practice 2    Dynamic Juggling, Passing and Receiving Practice

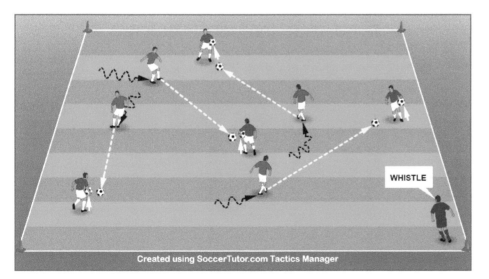

WHISTLE

**Description**

The red players dribble the ball around and the blue players are juggling.

On the coach's call, the blue players pick the ball up with their hands and at the same time receive a pass with their feet from the red players.

Players need to have awareness to look for a free player which stimulates a quick reading of the situation.

## Practice 3   Ball Control and Accurate Shooting Game

TOP RIGHT

Created using SoccerTutor.com Tactics Manager

### Description

Players dribble the ball through the cones and shoot within the square in the section of the goal called out by the coach:

1. Left.
2. Right
3. Middle.

### Variations

1. Dribble with only the inside or outside of foot.
2. Dribble with only the right or left foot.
3. Change the goal sections: Bottom left corner, top left corner, bottom right corner and top right corner.

## Practice 4   Technical Passing and Receiving in a Triangle

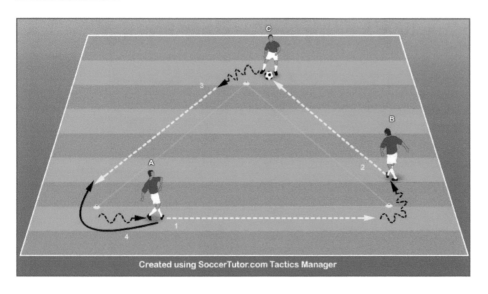

Created using SoccerTutor.com Tactics Manager

### Description

3 players pass the ball in a triangle.

Player A passes to B, who opens up and dribbles the ball round the cone. Player B then passes to C who does the same.

Finally, the ball is passed back to player A who has moved to the other side of the cone to receive.

### Variations

1. Change the type of pass (part of foot).
2. Change how the players receive the ball and dribble.
3. Change the geometric shape from triangle to another shape.

## Practice 5  Ball Control Practice in Pairs

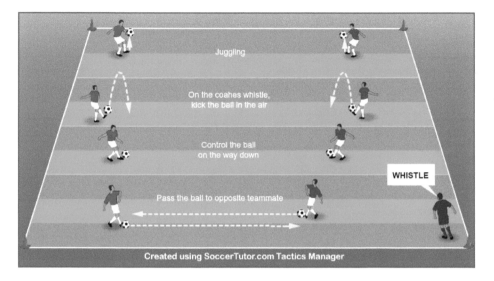

### Description

Players work in pairs with a ball each and wait for the coach's whistle.

At the whistle, the players kick the ball high up in the air, control it and then exchange passes with their teammate.

### Variation

Change the way to receive the ball and to pass the ball.

## Practice 6  Chip Pass, Receive and Shoot in a Team Game

### Description

We practice receiving the ball, dribbling and shooting.

The player on the touch line chips the ball into the square.

The player in the square receives the pass, dribbles the ball forward into to the shooting zone (marked by traffic cones) and shoots in the goal.

### Variations

1. Change the type of pass (part of foot).
2. Change how the players receive the ball and dribble.
3. Change the geometric shape from triangle to another shape.

# Balance

**Changing Direction and Receiving Relay**

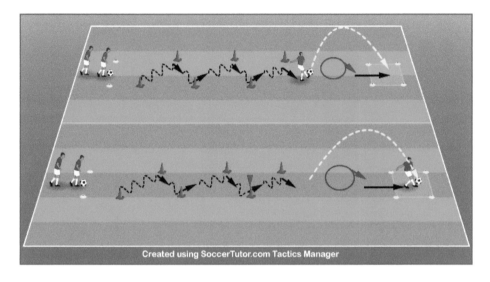

Created using SoccerTutor.com Tactics Manager

### Description

The player runs with the ball at high speed with quick changes of direction between the cones (as shown in the diagram).

They then kick the ball up in the air, do a forward roll and then control the ball inside the box.

The next player then goes and they return to the start.

---

**Crossing and Finishing Practice with Volleys and Headers**

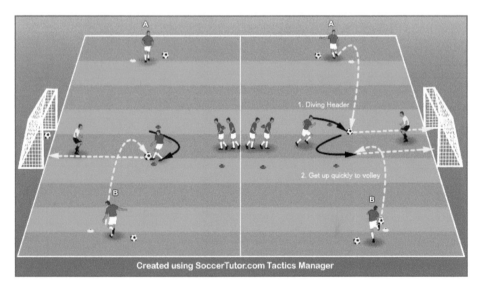

1. Diving Header

2. Get up quickly to volley

Created using SoccerTutor.com Tactics Manager

### Description

The players line up to finish on goal against the goalkeeper. At the sides, there are 2 players who cross the ball in for them (A and B).

When A crosses the ball, the blue players use a diving header to score in the goal.

When B crosses, the blue player quickly gets up off the ground to volley the second ball in the goal.

### Variation

Acrobatic volley.

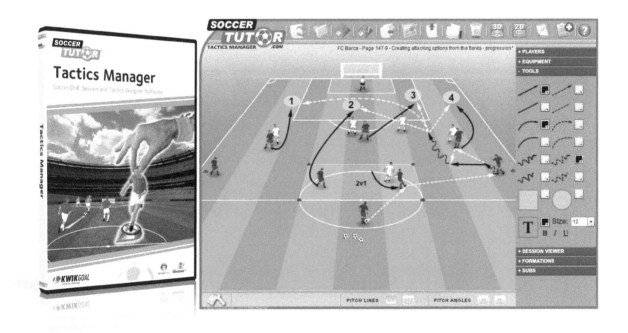